THE LIFE

OF

SIR ISAAC NEWTON.

> " ———— Newton, child-like sage !
> Sagacious reader of the works of God,
> And in His word sagacious."
>
> COWPER'S TASK.

PHILADELPHIA :

AMERICAN SUNDAY-SCHOOL UNION,

NO. 146 CHESTNUT STREET.

LONDON:

RELIGIOUS TRACT SOCIETY.

First printing: January 2014

For information write:
New Leaf Publishing Group, P.O. Box 726, Green Forest, AR 72638.
Attic Books is a division of the New Leaf Publishing Group, Inc.

ISBN-13: 978-0-89051-796-3

Library of Congress Number: 2013956459

Printed in the United States of America

Please visit our website for other great titles: www.nlpg.com

Originally published in 1907 by the American Sunday-school Union
(ASSU) in partnership with the London Religious Tract Society. With
its roots in the latter part of the 1700s, the ASSU, now called InFaith,
sent missionaries with books published by the mission to leave with
fledgling Sunday schools they had started, promoting literacy, education,
and the very best in Christian moral values.

Publisher's note: In order to preserve the historical nature of this work,
the British spellings and formatting of the text have been carefully
reproduced as they were in the original book.

CONTENTS.

CHAPTER I.

CHAPTER II.

CHAPTER III.

CHAPTER IV.

CHAPTER V.

CONTENTS

p93

p/72-173

LIFE

SIR ISAAC NEWTON.

CHAPTER I.

Eminent men in science during the sixteenth and seventeenth centuries—Birth of Newton—Youthful promise—Grantham school—Scientific amusements

THE interest which has belonged to the name of Newton throughout the civilized world for nearly two hundred years, is built on foundations so solid, that no person can be regarded as even tolerably well informed, who has not some acquaintance with the works of this most illustrious of natural philosophers. An exact acquaintance with those works must ever be confined to the learned few ; by them they are always esteemed in proportion to the extent and accuracy of their own acquirements in those departments of science to which Newton has added so much lustre.

We purpose, in this volume, to present a continuous narrative of the chief occurrences in Newton's life, and such an account of his mental labours, his discoveries, and his writings, as may both amuse and instruct the reader.

It will be difficult to understand what Newton was, and what he did, without having before us a general idea of the state of science when he appeared, especially the discoveries which had been made in astronomy and in optics. It will materially aid us, also, to have some familiarity with the other philosophers of the same age, with whom it is fair to compare Newton, and who were useful to him, either in encouraging his early studies, in bringing him out from the retirement to which his modesty would have confined him, or in calling the attention of the scientific world to his extraordinary inventions and productions.

ROGER BACON, the light of England in the thirteenth century, had astonished his fellow-countrymen with *suggestions* in physical science, to be fully carried out in succeeding generations; and the labours of not a few continental scholars had extended a portion of their fame to the more cultivated minds in this nation.

In the sixteenth century, COPERNICUS, born at Thorn in Prussia, abandoned the pursuit of medicine, to study astronomy with Dominic Maria at Bologna, and afterwards to teach mathematics in Rome. Copernicus was nephew to the bishop of Ermeland, who made him a canon of the cathedral at Frauenberg. While carrying on his astronomical observations in a house well situated on the brow of a hill, he devoted a large portion of his time to the examination of ancient opinions on the system of the universe. After comparing the various schemes for thirty years, he reached the discovery that *the sun is the centre of our system.* This great truth, and others connected with it, he established in his " Revolutions of the Heavenly Bodies." Slowly and cautiously he overturned the established opinions of mankind. Nine years after the writing of his book, he was prevailed on by George Rheticus, mathematical professor at Wirtemberg, to allow him to publish some account of his system, and his own work was printed at Nuremberg. A complete copy was handed to him in his last moments, and he saw and touched it a few hours before his death.*

Three years after Copernicus died, Tycho Brahe, of a Swedish family, was born at Knudstorp, in Norway. At the age of fourteen, while a student at Copenhagen, an eclipse of

* Brewster's Life of Newton, p. 118.

the sun, which had been predicted, engaged his
attention, and he was filled with an insatiable
thirst for so infallible a science.   To escape the
reproaches and even persecutions which his new
studies brought upon him, he left Denmark to
travel in Germany.   At Rostock he encountered
a Danish nobleman, like himself a mathematician, but, like himself, also, of hasty temper, and
they agreed to determine a dispute in geometry
by an appeal to the sword!   Tycho lost the
greater part of his nose in the duel.   At Augs-
burg, Peter Hainzell, the *burgomeister* of the
city, built an observatory, where the Danish
astronomer laid the foundations of his imperish-
able fame.   In a few years, he was received at
court by the king of Denmark, honoured by all
ranks, and encouraged to the utmost in the
prosecution of his studies ; there he had the
remarkable advantage of observing the new
star in Cassiopeia, which was visible for many
months, even in the daytime.   From Denmark
Tycho removed to Basle ; but his sovereign
induced him, by extraordinary munificence, to
return, and for twenty years he continued to
enlarge the boundaries of science at Uranibourg.
The observatory in which he carried on his
observations cost the king about £20,000.   In
this royal retreat he was visited by James I. of

England who paid him the highest compliments in his power. Tycho was an *observer*, not a philosophical reasoner. He rejected the system of Copernicus. The death of his sovereign left Tycho at the mercy of his enemies at court, and he was driven with his wife and children into exile. At Prague, he enjoyed the protection and the bounty of the emperor Rodolph II.

The agonies of Tycho's dying bed were soothed by the conversation of his illustrious disciple, JOHN KEPLER. Kepler was born at Wiel, in Wirtemberg, in 1571. His earlier days were spent in the service of the church ; but he was little more than twenty-three years old when he was called to the mathematical chair at Gratz, in Styria. In two years, he published a speculative work. It was condemned by Tycho Brahe, who advised him to *begin his philosophy with observation.* He succeeded his master in the favour of the emperor, and continued to enjoy the imperial patronage of Rodolph's successors, Matthias and Ferdinand. Tycho had discovered the *variation* of the moon's motion, her annual *equation*, and the *inclinations* of her orbit. Kepler came into the possession of Tycho's invaluable observations ; and while trying, by their means, the theory of the uniform circular motion of the planets, he arrived at the discovery, that "Mars revolves round the sun, *not* in a circular, but in an *elliptical* orbit." He also made, by means of these observations, the equally important discovery in physical astronomy — that " the radius vector describes equal areas in equal times." These discoveries were gradually established as including all the other planets in the solar system, and they were published in Kepler's " Commentaries on the Motions of the Planet Mars, as deduced from the Observations of Tycho Brahe." After much fruitless speculation, and many anxious but erroneons calculations, he discovered the great law, "that the squares of the periodic times of any two planets are to one another as the cubes of their distances from the sun." When he made this discovery, he says, he at first believed that he was dreaming, and had taken for granted the very truth of which he was in search. The work in which he published it, " Harmony of the World," was dedicated to James VI. of Scotland.

These are the celebrated " Three Laws of Kepler :"—(1) " The motion of the planets in elliptical orbits ; (2) the proportion of the areas described, with the *time* in which they are described ; (3) the relations of the *squares* of the periodic times to the *cubes* of the distances."

Kepler's active mind propounded many sagacious *conjectures* respecting the sun as the centre of gravitation, the reciprocal law of gravitation itself, and its effect on the tides and on the irregularities of the moon's motions.

Contemporary with Kepler, but in another country, was GALILEO, a native of Pisa, and professor of mathematics at Padua. He had attained his forty-fifth year before he distinguished himself as an astronomical discoverer. The year in which Kepler published his " Commentary," Galileo was at Venice, where he heard of a new instrument for celestial observations. Without seeing it, he discovered the principle on which it was made. He then constructed one for himself, which, by subsequent experiments, he gradually improved into a telescope of sufficient power to " show things almost a thousand times larger, and above thirty times nearer to the naked eye."

The discoveries which this magnificent invention opened to Galileo were most brilliant. The four satellites of Jupiter were observed. A new analogy to our own planet was established. The path of Venus round the sun was traced in its varying phases. The rotation of the sun was deduced from the spots seen upon his disc. Mountains were beheld in the moon, and

her *libration* was ascertained.   Portions of the
ring of Saturn were observed.   Stars in the
Milky Way were proved to be at immeasur-
able distances, from their not being magnified
by the telescope.   The great system of Copernicus, according to which the planets move
around a central sun, was established beyond
controversy.

In the plenitude of his success and of his
reputation, Galileo naturally expected that the
system which Copernicus had made public,
with the highest sanctions of the church, would
be universally embraced by all lovers of truth,
and especially by Christians.   But he was de-
ceived.   In that liberal age—when the light of
science was banishing from the mind of Europe
so many errors of past times ; when the light of
Divine truth was unveiled by the Reformers ;
when the doctrine of *salvation by faith in Jesus
Christ without the deeds of the law*, was eagerly
embraced by thousands in the northern nations
—in that very age, the most enlightened Roman
Catholic in the world was cited before " the
Holy Inquisition," on a charge of heresy !   He
was accused of " maintaining as true the *false*
doctrine held by many, that the sun was im-
movable in the centre of the world, and that
the earth revolved with a diurnal motion ; of

having certain disciples, to whom he taught
the same doctrine; of keeping up a correspondence on the subject with several *German*
mathematicians; of having published letters
on the solar spots, in which he explained the
same doctrine as true; and of having glossed
over, with a false interpretation, the passages of
Scripture which were urged against it." These
" false opinions" he was required to renounce
altogether, or be cast into prison. In the presence of the great cardinal Bellarmine, Galileo
promised obedience, and he was dismissed. But
six years had not passed away before he published his " Cosmical System; or, Dialogues on
the two great Systems of the World, the Ptole-
mean and the Copernican." The Inquisition
saw that the obnoxious doctrines were gaining
ground, and they summoned the venerable
philosopher, now bending beneath the weight
of seventy years, to answer for his disobedience.
They condemned him to the prison of the Inquisition, *during pleasure,* and to the weekly
recital of the seven penitential psalms for three
years. The poor old man degraded himself,
and dishonoured the God of truth, by signing
an abjuration, and on his knees, with his right
hand on the Gospels, he cursed the truths which
God had honoured him to teach. If it be true,

as we are told, that, on rising from his knees, he said, "It does move, though," our sorrow is only the deeper, that so great a teacher should have been so moved by fear, or by superstition, to belie his conscience; while we are forced to express, as calmly as we may, our detestation of the tyrannous hypocrisy of a church which would demand the sacrifice, or accept it.

The Inquisition, however, had not all its own way. The Copernican system was expounded and defended by a Carmelite monk, under the sanction of a pious nobleman of Naples. Galileo, indeed, lay, unpitied by "the master spirits of the age," in the cell of the Inquisition. His imprisonment was relieved and shortened through the influence of the grand duke of Tuscany, and other illustrious courtiers. Broken by disease and by domestic sorrow, the last use he made of his failing sight was to observe the interesting astronomical phenomenon of the moon's *libration*, which he partially explained. His last days were comforted by some relaxation in the rigour of his punishment. Nearly deaf, and totally blind, he was seized with palpitation and fever, while actively studying the forces of percussion. After a few weeks of illness, he died, at the age of seventy-eight, in the same year in which Newton was born.

Other names deserve to be recorded among
the precursors of Newton in astronomical discovery. These were troublous times in England. " Yet, under circumstances so unpro-
pitious, it is instructive to contemplate the
picture presented to us, of a small band of
philosophers struggling against every disadvantage, pursuing their researches in seclusion,
obscurity, and neglect." There was William
Millbourne, in the village of Brancepeth, near
Durham, a humble curate, detecting errors in
the best astronomical tables then existing.
There was W. Gascoyne, a young country
gentleman, of Middleton, in Yorkshire, (who
was killed in the battle of Marston Moor,) the
inventor of the invaluable *micrometer*. There
was Crabtree, at Broughton, near Manchester.
There was Horrox, "in the rural hamlet of
Toxteth, near a small seaport town in Lancashire, called Liverpool," struggling through
poverty and neglect to Emanuel College, Cambridge, and returning to his native county, to
observe, *for the first time* by man, the transit of
Venus over the sun's disc, while a hard-work-
ing curate, on a " poor pittance," at Hool, near
Preston—a man of the highest order of genius.
There was William Oughtred, fellow of King's
College, and rector of Albury, " the mathematical oracle of his day."

In those disturbed times, Wilkins, Boyle, Wallis, Seth Ward, and their scientific associates, formed a philosophical society, first in London, and then in Oxford. JOHN FLAMSTEAD, a sickly lad at Derby, was employing his forced leisure in those unassisted studies of astronomy which have done so much to unveil the stars, and to make the ocean the high road of nations. Bouillard, in France, wrote the precious sentence, that "if attraction existed, *it would decrease as the square of the distance.*" At Naples, Borelli wrote a volume, to prove that the planets perform their motions round the sun *according to a general law.* Dr. Hooke instructed the Royal Society in the outline of the great comprehensive truth which it was the glory of Newton to *simplify* and *to demonstrate.**

ISAAC NEWTON was the only son of Isaac Newton and Harriet Ayscough. He was born on the 25th December, (o.s.) 1642, at the manor-house of Woolsthorpe, in the parish of Colsterworth, six miles south of Grantham, in Lincolnshire. The Newtons appear to have been anciently a Lancashire family, where

* Historical Essay on the first publication of Sir Isaac Newton's Principia. By Professor Rigaud.—Correspondence of Scientific Men of the Seventeenth Century.—Sir Isaac Newton and his Contemporaries. Edinburgh Review, No. cxlviii.

the name of the place, either taken or given by them, still remains. The house at Woolsthorpe was repaired about fifty years ago by the proprietor, Mr. Turner, of Stoke Rocheford, the author of "Collections for the History of the Town and Stoke of Grantham;" and in the chamber where Newton was born he placed a white marble tablet, with this inscription :—

"Sir Isaac Newton, son of John Newton, lord of the manor of Woolsthorpe, was born in this room, on the 25th December, 1642.

> "'Nature and Nature's laws lay hid in night;
>   God said, "Let Newton be," and all was light.'"

The following lines have been written upon the house :—

> "Here Newton dawned, here lofty wisdom woke,
>   And to a wondering world divinely spoke.
>   If Tully glowed, when Phædrus' steps he trod,
>   Or Fancy formed Philosophy a god—
>   If sages still for Homer's birth contend,
>   The sons of science at this dome must bend.
>   All hail the shrine! all hail the natal day!
>   Cam boasts his noon—this COT his morning ray."[*]

This child was born after his father's death. As an infant, he was remarkable for his extreme smallness and delicacy. His mother cherished him with tender anxiety on the paternal estate, which, together with a property of her own, three miles distant, at Sewstern, in Leicestershire, was of the value of eighty pounds a year.

[*] Sir David Brewster's Life of Newton, pp. 343, 344.

When Isaac was three years old, Mrs. Newton was married to the reverend Barnabas Smith, rector of North Witham, near Woolsthorpe. From that time, the child was committed to the charge of his maternal grandmother.   After acquiring the rudiments of education at the day schools of Skillington and of Stoke, he was placed, in his twelfth year, at the public school in Grantham, then taught by Mr. Stokes, and he lived in the house of Mr. Clarke, apothecary, of Grantham.   His own confessions represent him as somewhat idle, and far behind his compeers, until he received a severe kick from the boy immediately above him, when he resolved to rise to the head of the school, and attained the object of his ambition by the habit of close application to study which he never abandoned. His amusements were not those of his companions.   He procured a number of saws, hammers, hatchets, and such other mechanical tools as he could handle, and soon learned to use them with great skill.   He made a carriage, to be moved by the person sitting in it.   He contrived a clock, which marked the time exactly by the falling of water.   A peculiar kind of windmill was built near the road from Grantham to Gunnerby; during its erection, Newton had watched the workmen so carefully, that he soon produced a model of it, which was seen at work on the top of Mr. Clarke's house, and was greatly admired. The ingenious contriver shut up a mouse in his little mill, calling it his *miller*. This industrious miller moved the machine, and ate up the flour. To divert his school-mates, Newton manufactured paper kites on the best scientific principles. In the dark mornings of winter, he carried with him paper lanterns, and at night he alarmed the ignorant neighbours with the dread of comets, by tying the lanterns to the tails of kites. He covered the walls of his apartment with mathematical figures, drawings from nature, or copies from designs. Some of these he had framed. Under a portrait of king Charles I. were some verses, believed to have been written by Newton himself :

> "A secret art my soul requires to try,
> If prayers can give me what the wars deny.
> Three crowns, distinguished here, in order do
> Present their objects to my knowing view.
> Earth's crown thus at my feet I can disdain,
> Which heavy is, and at the best but vain.
> But now a crown of thorns I gladly greet;
> Sharp is this crown, but not so sharp as sweet.
> The crown of glory that I yonder see,
> Is full of bliss and of eternity."

It is not unlikely that the imperfections which the young philosopher detected in his water-clock led him to pay more attention to the sun, whose apparent motions he marked out by pegs, which he placed at such distances as gave the hours and half-hours. It is related that, in the house where he lodged while at school, Newton was happy in the society of some young ladies, for whose convenience and gratification it was a pleasure to turn his mechanical ingenuity to account. With one of these ladies, his junior by two or three years, Miss Storey, who was afterwards twice married, he cultivated a lively friendship. This lady lived at Grantham to the age of eighty-two, and, after the death of Newton, communicated many interesting particulars of his early life to Dr. Stukely. These were published by Turner, in his " Collections for the History of the Town and Stoke of Grantham."

Newton's mother again became a widow, having had three daughters by the rector of North Witham. Leaving the rectory, she returned to the manor of Woolsthorpe, and recalled her son from Grantham to help her in the management of their little farm. He was now fifteen years old. He was regularly sent to the market at Grantham to dispose of their produce, and to make the purchases needed in the family. A trusty servant accompanied him on these occasions. When they had put up their horses at the Saracen's Head, Newton left the business to the servant, repaired to his old lodgings, and pursued his studies till the evening. Sometimes he did not go to Grantham at all, but occupied himself with his own thoughts in the shade of a hedge-row, until his faithful companion rejoined him on his return from market. " The more immediate affairs of the farm were not more prosperous under his management than would have been his marketings at Grantham. The perusal of a book, the execution of a model, or the superintendence of a water-wheel of his own construction, whirling the glittering spray from some neighbouring stream, absorbed all his thoughts when the sheep were going astray, and the cattle were devouring or treading down the corn." *

Mrs. Smith now perceived that the capacities, attainments, and habits of her son, were such as to encourage her to secure for him all the culture within his reach. She sent him back to Grantham school, where he spent several months in ardent study. His maternal uncle, the rector of a neighbouring parish, who had studied at Trinity College, Cambridge, persuaded him to enter the same society, to which it was finally resolved that he should proceed at the following term.

* Sir David Brewster's Life of Newton, p. 10.

CHAPTER II.

Isaac Newton was admitted sub-sizar at Trinity College on the 5th of June, 1661, in the twentieth year of his age. The class of students to which he belonged was "required to perform various menial services, which now seem to be considered degrading to a young man who is endeavouring by the force of his intellect to raise himself to his proper position in society."*

To prepare himself for the public lessons of the university, where a predilection for the elements of algebra and geometry had been growing for more than fifty years, Newton read the text-books beforehand. These were bishop Sanderson's "Compendium of Logic," and Kepler's "Optics." In addition to these text-books,

* Edleston's "Correspondence of Newton," p. 41.

he studied the " Geometry" of Des Cartes, and the
"*Arithmetica Infinitorum*" of Wallis. Before he
had been three years at Cambridge, he recorded
some observations on two halos round the
moon. About two months after, he was elected
scholar, and in the following winter he took his
degree as bachelor of arts. It is somewhat
curious that the " academical estimate formed
of the most illustrious candidate that ever
offered himself for a degree" cannot now be
ascertained, as " the ' *Ordo Senioritatis*' of the
bachelors of arts for this year is provokingly
omitted in the grace-book."* Within a few
weeks from the time of taking his first degree,
he composed some mathematical papers on
Fluxions, and their application to tangents, and
to the *curvature of curves*. In the following
year, he applied himself to the grinding of
optical glasses, of figures not spherical ; and,
having procured a triangular glass prism, he
discovered the *unequal refrangibility of light*. The
apparent hopelessness of perfecting the refracting telescope, induced him to give his attention
to reflectors. But the plague broke out at Cambridge at that time, and he retired to his native
manor of Woolsthorpe. He took his degree of
master of arts in 1668, having been previously

* Note by Edleston, p. 41.

elected, first to a *minor*, and then to a *major* fellowship. The year after, he succeeded Dr. Isaac Barrow in the mathematical professorship founded by Mr. Lucas. This was the period at which Newton made those grand discoveries which raised him to the highest place in the highest walks of human intellect.

The most inquisitive philosophers were, at that time, engaged in studying the nature of light, with a special view to astronomical observations. Till then it had been universally believed that every colour of light was *equally* refracted when passing through a lens, or any other refracting medium. Newton determined to analyse the exhibition of colours by the prism. He made a hole in his window-shutter, and, having darkened the chamber, he let a portion of the sun's light, entering by the hole, pass through a triangular prism. The various colours formed an image on the opposite wall, which was *five times as long as it was broad.* When he had seen with delight the vivid colours thus produced, he was curious to learn how it came to pass that while the white image of the sunbeam was *circular*, the image of the many-coloured beam which had passed through the prism was so much longer than it was broad. Having satisfied himself by careful experiments that the length of the image was not caused by any irregularity in the glass of the prism, by any differences in the incidence of light from different parts of the sun's disk, or by any curvature in the direction of the rays, he was led to the important conclusion that light is *not homogeneous*, or of one and the same kind of substance, but consists of rays of different refrangibility—the *red* being less refracted than the *orange;* the orange less refracted than the *yellow;* and the *violet* more refracted than any of the other rays. The application of this discovery to telescopes was of great practical importance ; while rays of light passing through a glass lens were *refracted* with varying degrees of force, and thus produced indistinctness of vision, Newton found that rays of all colours were regularly *reflected,* and, for this reason, he bent his mind, after his return to Cambridge, to the construction of *the first reflecting telescope* that was ever used in exploring the heavens. So great was the success of this little instrument, *only six inches long*, that he distinctly saw through it Jupiter and his four satellites, and the horns of Venus. A second telescope, made with his own hands, was shown to the king by members of the Royal Society, in the library of the society.

The telescope is preserved, with this inscription :—

"Invented by sir Isaac Newton, and made with his own hands, 1671."[*]

Newton had delivered his great discoveries relating to light in a course of lectures on *optics* at Cambridge, which continued from 1669 till 1671. The manuscript table of these lectures is preserved in the university library at Cambridge. They are sixteen in number, and contain his grand discoveries relating to light. After the presentation of his telescope to the Royal Society, he was proposed by Dr. Seth Ward, lord bishop of Salisbury, as a Fellow of the society. In a letter to Oldenburg, the secretary, he says : " I am very sensible of the honour done me by the bishop of Sarum, in proposing me as a candidate, and which I hope will be further conferred upon me by my election into the society ; and if so, I shall endeavour to testify my gratitude by communicating what my poor and solitary endeavours can effect towards the promoting your philosophical designs." In another letter to the secretary, he

[*] " The instrument in Trinity College library, which is usually shown to visitors as Newton's own telescope, I believe to have belonged to Robert Smith, and to be that which is described in his 'Optics,' p. 304, note. The inscription upon 'Sir Isaac Newton's telescope,' merely means a Newtonian telescope."—Edleston, p. 45.

writes: " I desire that in your next letter you would inform me for what time the society continue their weekly meetings ; because, if they continue them for any time, I am purposing them to be considered and examined, *an* account of *a philosophical discovery, which induced me to the making of the said telescope; and I doubt not but will prove much more grateful than the communication of that instrument, being, in my judgment, the oddest fact, the most considerable detection which hath hitherto been made* in the operations of nature."

At the request of the Royal Society, Newton published these, and other discoveries relating to colours, in the Transactions of the Society. In the course of these papers he proved that *white* light is a compound of all the seven prismatic colours. The method of demonstrating this truth cannot be exactly explained without diagrams. The one which will be most easily understood by a description in words is thus given by sir David Brewster: " It consisted in attempting to compound a white by mixing the coloured powders used by painters. He was aware that such colours, from their very nature, could not compose a pure white ; but even this imperfection in the experiment he removed by an ingenious device. He accordingly mixed one part of *red lead*, four parts of *blue bise*, and a proper proportion of *orpiment*, (yellow,) and *verdigris*, (green.) This mixture was *dun*, like wood newly cut, or like the human skin. He now took one kind of the mixture, and rubbed it thickly on the floor of his room, where the sun shone upon it through the open casement, and beside it, in the shadow, he laid a piece of white paper of the same size. Then going from them to the distance of twelve or eighteen feet, so that he could not discern the unevenness of the surface of the powder, nor the little shadows let fall from the gritty particles thereof, the powder appeared intensely white, so as to transcend even the paper itself in whiteness. By adjusting the relative illuminations of the powders and the paper, he was able to make them both appear of the very same degree of whiteness. ' For,' says he, ' when I was trying this, a friend coming to visit me, I stopped him at the door, and before I told him what the colours were, or what I was doing, I asked him which of the two whites were the best, and wherein they differed ; and after he had, at that distance, viewed them well, he answered that they were both good whites, and that he could not say which was best, or wherein their colours differed.' Hence Newton inferred that perfect whiteness may be compounded of different colours."

Besides the discovery of the different degrees of refrangibility in rays of different colours, and the composition of colours in producing white, he arrived at the further conclusion—that the *colours of natural bodies are not inherent qualities, but are produced by the capacity of the particles to absorb certain rays, and to reflect the others.*

These beautiful discoveries were opposed by Pardies, a Jesuit professor of mathematics at Clermont, and by Linus, a physician at Liege ; but to each of these opponents Newton gave clear and triumphant replies. He was involved in a more painful controversy with Dr. Hooke and with Christian Huyghens, both of them eminent philosophers ; though he had the satisfaction of humbling his antagonists in argument, he said, " I intend to be no further solicitous about matters of philosophy, and therefore, I hope you will not take it ill if you find me never doing anything more in that kind, or rather that you will favour me in my determination, by preventing, so far as you can conveniently, any objections or other philosophical letters that may concern me." " I have some thoughts of writing a further discourse about colours, to be read at one of your assem-

blies, but find it yet against the grain to put
pen to paper any more on the subject." "I was
so persecuted with discussions arising from my
theory of light, that I blamed my own impru-
dence for parting with so substantial a blessing
as my quiet to run after a shadow." Newton's
theory of *fits of easy reflexion and transmission*
of light was suggested by the examination of
the colours of extremely thin plates of mica.
His theory of the *colours of natural bodies* is one
of the most entertaining, though not the most
satisfactory of his wonderful speculations. He
explains *transparency* by supposing that the
particles of transparent bodies, and the pores
between them, are too small to cause reflexion
at their surfaces, so that the light *passes through*
them without any portion of it being *bent* from
its path. *Opacity* he explains by an opposite
condition of bodies, in which the light is *all*
bent from its course. *Colours* he explains by
representing the transparent particles of bodies
as *reflecting* rays of one colour, and *transmitting*
those of another. This theory, which is generally admitted, is, however, open to strong objections, which are very clearly and forcibly
stated by sir David Brewster, in the seventh
chapter of his Life of Newton. We have no
space here for discussions, and they do not

enter into our present design. It will be more interesting to the reader to give Brewster's introduction to that chapter.

" If the objects of the material world had been illuminated with white light, all the particles of which possessed the same degree of refrangibility, and were equally acted upon by the bodies on which they fall, *all nature would have shone with a leaden hue*, and all the combinations of external objects, and all the features of the human countenance, would have exhibited no other variety but that which they possess in a pencil-sketch or a China-ink drawing. The rainbow itself would have dwindled into a narrow arch of white light, the stars would have shone through a grey sky, and the mantle of a wintry twilight would have replaced the golden vesture of the rising and the setting sun. But He, who has exhibited such matchless skill in the organization of material bodies, and such exquisite taste in the forms upon which they are modelled, has *superadded that ethereal beauty which enhances their more permanent qualities*, and presents them to us in the ever varying colours of the spectrum. Without this the foliage of vegetable life might have filled the eye and fostered the fruit which it veils, but the youthful green of its spring

would have been blended with the dying yellow
of its autumn. Without this the diamond
might have displayed to science the beauty of
its forms, and yielded to the arts its adamantine
virtues ; but it would have ceased to shine in
the chaplet of beauty, and to sparkle in the
diadem of princes. Without this the human
countenance might have expressed all the
sympathies of the heart, but the 'purple light
of love' would not have risen on the cheek, nor
the hectic flush been the herald of its decay.

" The gay colouring with which the Almighty
has decked the pale marble of nature, is not the
result of any quality inherent in the coloured
body, or in the particles by which it may be
tinged, but is merely a property of the light in
which they happen to be placed. NEWTON *was
the first person* who placed this great truth in
the clearest evidence."

Before Newton directed his unrivalled powers
of observation to the inflexion of light, the
phenomena had been described by Grimaldi, an
Italian Jesuit, and Dr. Robert Hooke had communicated to the Royal Society of London the
doctrine of interference by which the phenomena are explained. The explanation given
by Newton is all that concerns us here. He
measured " the diameter of the shadow of a

human hair, and the breadth of the *fringes* at different distances behind it, when he discovered the remarkable fact, that these diameters and breadths were not proportional to the distances from the hair at which they were measured. In order to explain these phenomena, Newton supposed that *the rays which passed by the edge of the hair* are deflected or turned aside from it, *as if by a repulsive force*, the nearest rays suffering the greatest, and those remote a less degree of deflexion." He further supposed, that the rays which differ in refrangibility differ also in flexibility; that, by these different *inflections*, they are separated from each other; that, after their separation, they make different colours in the fringes seen on the shadows of objects; and that, in passing by the sides and edges of bodies, these rays form the fringes by being bent backwards and forwards several times, with a motion like that of an eel. Sir David Brewster, on the contrary, ascribes the phenomena in question, not, as Newton did, to the properties of bodies acting on light, but, as Hooke had done, to a property *in the light itself.*

The researches of Newton in connexion with " the double refraction of light," led him to reject the law expounded by Huyghens, and

confirmed by numerous experiments. But the
law which he substituted for that of Huyghens,
in the queries appended to his "Optics," has
been universally rejected.

From the successive appearance and re-ap-
pearance of two of the four images formed by
looking at a luminous object through two rhombs
of calcareous spar, the one turning round upon
the other, Newton concluded that each ray of
light has two opposite sides, endued with the
property of producing the double refraction,
and two other opposite sides which have not
that property. By comparing the *sides* of a
ray of light to the *poles* of a magnet, he seems
to have had no perception of the *polarity* of rays
of light.

Newton's "Treatise on Optics" was not published during Hooke's life. The jealousy on
the part of the latter of a rival so much superior to himself, had been the source of great
disquietude to Newton. It appeared in English
two years after the death of Hooke, and two
years afterwards in Latin. This Latin translation was made (with alterations and additions,
including seven new queries) by Samuel Clarke,
on which occasion Newton made him a present
of £500. A second edition was published in
1719. It forms a body of "Optics" so new,

that Fontenelle regards the science as almost
entirely due to the illustrious author. The
same writer says of the same work, that one
great advantage of it, as great perhaps as the
fulness of novel information with which it is
filled, is—that it furnishes an excellent model
of the art of conducting inquiries in experimental philosophy.

CHAPTER III.

WE have seen that the movements of the heavenly bodies had been determined by the discoveries of Copernicus ; that they moved in elliptical orbits, and that their periodic times were related to their distances from their centre ; that Galileo had laid open to the view of astronomers a wide variety of planetary revolutions; and that all their vast and complex movements had been referred by astronomers to attraction. With all these discoveries Newton was fully acquainted, and he was thus *prepared* for the grand discovery with which his name is identified. On his retirement from Cambridge, during the continuance of the plague, he was meditating on the power by which all bodies are made to descend to the earth. The story of the falling apple is well known. As it is not mentioned by Dr. Stukeley nor by Mr. Conduit,

and as no authority for it was found by sir
David Brewster, that exact and able writer did
not feel himself at liberty to use it. Professor
Regaud thought it was derived from unquestionable authority. Voltaire, in his " Elements
of the Philosophy of Newton," says that it is
attested by Mrs. Conduit, Newton's niece.
The *tradition* is religiously preserved upon the
spot, and the tree from which the apple fell
being destroyed in a storm in 1827, the timber
was made into a chair, which is still preserved.
It is spoken of by Biot, in the " *Journal des
Savans* " for 1832, the year after the publication of Brewster's Life of Newton ; and Green,
in his " Philosophy of Expansive and Contrac-
tive Forces," says that he received it from his
friend Martin Folkes. According to this tradition, it was the falling of the apple that led
Newton into the train of thought which ended
in his great discovery.

That apples fall from trees is a general fact
which it certainly did not need a Newton to
discover ; on the other hand, the *reason why*
they fall was as certainly not discovered by
Newton, nor, perhaps, will it be by any other
philosopher. But the great law of nature,
according to which they fall, though partly
guessed at by others, and that this law is the

same, and the unknown cause, (whatever it be,)
the same for apples as for planets, it is the
exclusive claim of Newton to have disclosed
and demonstrated. Yet somewhat perplexed
and mystified statements of the matter are occasionally made. In point of fact, Newton simply
reasoned thus:—If gravitation extend from
apples to the moon, it is perpetually drawing
the moon to the earth by the momentary
deflection of its curvilinear orbit from the direct
line of the tangent; and if it decrease as the
square of the distance increases, then, at the
distance of sixty times the earth's radius,
it ought to be the 3,600th part of the force
of gravity near the earth's surface, where
it makes bodies fall sixteen feet in a second. But, from the known period of the
moon, and dimensions of her orbit, the actual
deflexion can be calculated, dependent on the
value assigned to the earth's radius. Employing
the value derived from the commonly received
estimate of sixty miles to the degree, he found
the resulting actual deflexion considerably less
than the theory required. He consequently
desisted from the inquiry, and turned his
attention to other subjects. The share which
each of his predecessors in the attempt to solve
this question could fairly claim has been much

misapprehended. Horrox, Hooke, Huyghens, Halley, and Wren, had made *approaches towards it*, which are detailed by the writer of " Sir Isaac Newton and his Contemporaries," in the Edinburgh Review. The error in Newton's first calculation arose from his taking the radius of the earth according to the *received notion*, that a degree measured sixty miles, whereas Picard had determined it to be sixty-nine and a half miles. This was mentioned at a meeting of the Royal Society in 1682, at which Newton was present. " It immediately struck him that the value of the earth's radius was the erroneous element in his first calculation. With a feverish interest in this result, little imagined by those present, he hurried home, resumed his calculation with the new value, and having proceeded some way in it, was so overpowered by nervous agitation at its anticipated result, that he was unable to go on, and requested a friend to finish it for him, when it came out, *exactly establishing the inverse square* as the true measure of the moon's gravitation, and thus furnishing the key to the whole system." Such is the account of the matter given by Pemberton, enlarged by Robinson, and adopted by Biot. Some dates and circumstantial particulars are corrected by the writer in the Edinburgh Review, already quoted ; but the fact that the error of the first calculation was corrected by Picard's determination of the *true* value of the degree is beyond all doubt.

Dr. Hooke and Dr. Halley had both attempted to demonstrate the laws of the celestial motions. Hooke declared that he possessed the true method, which he intended for some time to keep to himself. Dr. Halley went to Cambridge in August, 1684, to consult Newton on the subject, and he was assured by Newton that he had himself completed the demonstration, of which he promised him a copy. Before the end of April, in the following year, the manuscript, entitled "*Philosophiæ Naturalis Principia Mathematica*," was presented by Dr. Vincent to the Royal Society.

This " brightest page in the history of human reason" is divided into three books. The first and second books relate to " The Motion of Bodies." The third is on the " System of the World." Three-fourths of the work are filled with the " Mathematical Principles," in their relation to the laws and conditions of motions and forces, illustrating the density of bodies, spaces void of matter, and the motions of sound and light. In the third book he has drawn up, in a style suited to general readers, the consti-

tution of the world, as deduced from the fore-
going principles. The great PRINCIPLE of the
system is—*that every particle of matter is attracted by, or gravitates to, every other particle
of matter, with a force inversely proportioned to
the squares of their distances.*

This great law was established, not only by
mathematical reasoning, but by accurate experiments. By means of these he was able to determine the *curve* in which a body moves when
acted on by a force which varies inversely with
the squares of the distance ; the action of sphere
on sphere ; the gravitation of the sun to the
planets, of the planets to their satellites, and of
the earth to the stone that falls upon it ; the
respective densities of the earth and other
planets, and of the sun ; the centrifugal force
which combines with the centripetal (gravitating) to preserve the balance of motion round
the centre ; the varying weight of bodies at
the poles and at the equator ; the true theory
of the tides, as depending on the relative position of the earth and the moon ; the explanation of the inequalities or variation of the
moon's motion ; the precession of the equi-
noctial through the circuit of the heavens in
25,920 years ; and the form, position, and
time of the motion of comets.

This extraordinary book, Newton says he wrote in about seventeen or eighteen months, of which about two were taken up in journeyings. Most writers would have required all the time for *preparing* such materials, even if they had been previously collected. The author must have had the main doctrines in his mind long before. To him they had become obvious truths. It was not until repeatedly urged by his friends that he consented to their publication. To Dr. Halley, pre-eminently, the world is indebted for the appearance of the "Principia." Though the Royal Society ordered the printing of the book, its actual publication was owing to the zeal, disinterestedness, and eminent scientific attainments of Dr. Halley. Newton himself was too fond of retirement and repose to be willing to encounter controversy. This unwillingness resulted mainly from that *unity* which seems to be peculiar to the highest order of minds —the calm consciousness of truth and power.

It would be a great mistake to infer from what has been said, that Newton merely dealt in sagacious *conjectures* which happened to be true, or that his discoveries *came to him* like dreams. He used extraordinary temperance, for the sake of preserving the clearness of his mind for study ; and, while engaged in his great discoveries, " he confined himself to a small quantity of bread during all the time, with a little sack and water." When he was asked by what means he had arrived at his discoveries, he answered, " By always *thinking to them*." On another occasion he said, " I keep the subject constantly before me, and wait till the first dawnings open slowly, by little and little, into a full and clear light." In a letter to Dr. Bentley he says, " If I have done the public any service this way, it is due to nothing but industry and patient thought." At the first publication of the " Principia," even the learned world was taken by surprise. The reasonings were so profound, the conclusions so novel, the system at once so simple, so grand, so comprehensive, so utterly subversive of theories previously maintained, that there were exceedingly few persons that even *understood* it. Others were prejudiced by their attachment to the prevailing philosophy of Des Cartes. The great French astronomer, Laplace, who thoroughly comprehended the " Principia," and who himself expounded the law of gravitation in *all* the movements of the celestial bodies, has nobly said : " Newton has well established the existence of the principle which he had the merit of discovering but the development of

its consequences and advantages has been the
work of the successors of this great mathematician.   The imperfection of the infinitesimal
calculus when first discovered, did not allow
him completely to resolve the difficult problems
which the theory of the universe offers ; and
he was oftentimes forced to give mere hints,
which were always uncertain till confirmed by
rigorous analysis.   Notwithstanding these unavoidable defects, the importance and the generality of his discoveries respecting the system
of the universe, and the most interesting points
of natural philosophy, the great number of
profound and original views, which have been
the origin of the most brilliant discoveries of
the mathematicians of the last century, which
were all presented with much elegance, will
insure to the *Principia a lasting pre-eminence
over all other productions of the human mind*."

Though the philosophy of Newton was opposed by the Cartesians, by Leibnitz, by
Huyghens, Mairan, Cassini, and Maraldi, it
was introduced to the universities of Holland
by S'Gravesande and Maupertius, and adopted
by the Chevalier Louville at Paris.   Its introduction to his own university of Cambridge
was by the notes of Dr. Samuel Clarke on a
Cartesians text-book, in which " Notes" he

explained the views of Newton in a way which, without the appearance of disputation, exposed the errors of the text. Newton himself had previously given his own doctrines from his own chair, as Lucasian professor. He was succeeded in that chair by Whiston, who carried out the same doctrines ; and the next successor, Sanderson, the blind mathematician, gained his popularity, and his appointment at Cambridge, by lecturing on the works of Newton. Dr. Samuel Clarke defended it in the public schools, and Dr. Laughton, proctor of Clare Hall, had promoted the same object with the utmost ardour. Roger Cotes, a disciple of Newton and his friend, diffused his principles by lecturing, and by publishing, with an excellent preface, a second edition of the "Principia." Dr. Bentley, master of Trinity College, not only encouraged the Newtonian philosophy at Cambridge, but introduced it to the general literature of Europe. At Oxford, it was pro pounded by professor Keil; at Edinburgh, by David Gregory, who afterwards taught it at Oxford ; at St. Andrew's, by James, brother of David Gregory. Its physical truths were taught, for the first time in public, not only in Oxford, but also in London, by Dr. John Keil.

" From the time of the publication of the

' Principia,' its mathematical doctrines formed regular parts of academical education ; and, before twenty years had elapsed, its physical truths were communicated to the public in popular lectures, illustrated by experiments, and accommodated to the capacities of those who were not versed in mathematical knowledge. The Cartesian system, though it may have lingered for a while in the recesses of our universities, was soon overturned; and, long before his death, Newton enjoyed the high satisfaction of seeing his philosophy triumphant in his native land." *

* Brewster's Life of Newton, p. 180.

CHAPTER IV.

Mathematical studies — The Binomial Theorem—Fluxions—
Universal arithmetic — Differential method — Geometrical
analysis—Problems of Bernouilli and of Leibnitz—Controversy respecting the discovery of fluxions.

It is only a mathematical reader that understands the invaluable discoveries, in that wide
and fascinating department of intellectual activity, with which Newton has enriched the world;
yet they form so important a part of his life,
that it is necessary some notice should here be
taken of them. Any reader may comprehend
the difference between a figure composed of
straight lines and angles, and a figure *contained
within* a *circle*, or any other curved line. The
method of finding out the quantity of space in
a figure of the former kind is obvious; and
the ancient geometers had adopted a method of
bringing a curve as near to a straight line as
possible, by drawing straight lines from one
point of the curve to another, until they had
reached that which left the smallest quantity of

space between the straight line and the curve,
something like the shortest possible string across
a bow. The space thus left between the straight
line and the curve (as between the string and
the bend of the bow) afforded the means of
constructing triangles continually decreasing in
size. The process of doing this was called the
method of *exhaustion*, the principle on which it
was done received the name of *infinite quantities*,
and the quantity of space measured was called
the area of the curve. Supposing quantities to be
infinitely small, a line may be conceived of
an infinite number of points, a surface as an
infinite number of lines, and a solid as an infinite
number of surfaces. The application of " infinite quantities" to the measurement of curves,
had engaged the attention of Roberval and
Fermat, Hudde, Huyghens, Barrow, Wallis, and
Kauffman, all of whom had made a near
approach to the famous problem of squaring
the circle. This was a branch of science which
could not fail to interest the mind of Newton.
By the *Binomial Theorem*, which he discovered
in pursuing these studies, he had reached the
shortest method of reducing curves to squares,
and of solving some of the most difficult questions in mathematics.

By considering lines as points in motion, and

surfaces as lines in motion, he ascertained the
velocities with which these motions were performed, calling the lines *fluents* and the velocities *fluxions*.   These discoveries, of incalculable
value in mathematical investigations, and in the
study of astronomy, were made by Newton
before the plague drove him from Cambridge.
He had communicated them more or less fully
in private correspondence, and had given the
fundamental principle in his " Principia." His
dread of controversy prevented his publishing
the entire " Method," which appeared for the
first time in an English translation after his
death ; other mathematical works, however,
bearing on the same general subject, were published with his consent during his life.

In 1697, Bernouilli challenged the ablest
mathematicians in the world to solve two problems on curved lines, allowing six months for
the solution.   Leibnitz obtained a delay of
twelve months.   The solution was given by
Leibnitz, by the Marquis de l'Hopital, and by
Newton.   Newton sent his solution of both the
problems to Mr. Charles Montague, the president of the Royal Society, *on the day after* he
had received them ; and though it was anony-
mous, Bernouilli recognised the author.

In 1716, Leibnitz proposed an extremely

difficult problem, "for the purpose of feeling the pulse of the English analysts." Newton received it in the evening, as he was going home from the Mint, and solved it before he retired to rest.

The unwillingness of Newton to publish his discoveries appears to have been the occasion of the most harassing of the controversies which he was most anxious to avoid. Leibnitz had certainly anticipated him in *publishing his* discoveries in fluxions, and it was insinuated that Newton had stolen his method from Leibnitz. This accusation gave rise to a long and irritating dispute between the advocates of Leibnitz on the one hand, and of Newton on the other, until it assumed the seriousness of personal quarrel, and even of national jealousy. We believe the truth to be, that both Newton and Leibnitz were, independently of each other, *inventors* of fluxions ; that Newton was the *first* inventor, but that Leibnitz was the first who gave the invention to the world.

CHAPTER V.

Newton's public life—James II. and the university of Cam-
bridge—Newton in parliament—Appointed Warden of the
Mint—Favour at court—Republication of the " Principia"—
Works on chronology.

In February, 1687, James II. directed a royal
letter to the university of Cambridge, requiring
that Alban Francis, a Benedictine monk, should
be admitted Master of Arts. According to the
law of the university, the oaths of allegiance
and supremacy were required in such a case.
Francis refused to take these oaths ; and, as the
officers declined admitting him in violation of
the law, he went to Whitehall to complain of
their disloyalty to the king. James would
accept of no explanation from the heads of the
colleges, but summoned the vice-chancellor and
the senate before the new High Commission.
Among the deputies sent by the senate was
Isaac Newton. "His genius was then in the
fullest vigour. The great work, which entitles
him to the highest place among the geometri-

cians and natural philosophers of all ages and nations, had been some time printing with the sanction of the Royal Society, and was almost ready for publication. He was the steady friend of civil liberty and of the Protestant religion ; but his habits by no means fitted him for the conflicts of active life. He therefore stood modestly silent among the delegates, and left to men more versed in practical business the task of pleading the cause of his beloved university."* The firm stand taken by the delegates prevailed, and Francis was rejected. Dr. Lingard, the Roman Catholic historian of England, affects to treat this as a trifling matter. Newton and his associates justly regarded it as involving a deep constitutional question between the arbitrary will of the monarch and the law of the land.

Although Newton had taken only a silent part in the defence of the university, and of the civil and religious liberties of Englishmen, his conduct in this delicate business, and his general reputation, secured his election to represent the university in the Convention parliament of 1688.

His attendance on parliamentary duties

* Macaulay's History of England, from the accession of James II., p. 282. Third Edition.

required his residence in London, but the books of the university record his presence at Cambridge during the greater part of the years from 1689 to 1695. At this period, Newton had no source of revenue beyond the small rent of his property in Lincolnshire, and the salary of his office as mathematical professor. Charles Montague, afterwards the famous earl of Halifax, was a personal friend of Newton's at Cambridge, and he had been a member of the same parliament. When raised to the post of chancellor of the exchequer, Montague found the coin of the realm greatly debased, and, amidst much opposition, he resolved on issuing a new coinage. On this important subject, he had held communications with Locke, Halley, and Newton, the latter of whom he recommended to the office of warden of the Mint. The appointment was reported to Newton in the following letter :—

"London, 19th March, 1695.

" Sir,—I am very glad that at last I can give you a good proof of my friendship and the esteem the king has of your merits. Mr. Overton, the warden of the Mint, is made one of the commissioners of the Customs, and the king has promised me to make Mr. Newton warden of the Mint. The office is the most proper for you. 'Tis the chief office in the

Mint; 'tis worth five or six hundred pounds
per annum, and has not too much business to
require more attention than you can spare. I
desire that you will come up as soon as you can,
and I will take care of your warrant in the mean-
time. Let me see you as soon as you come to
town, that I may carry you to kiss the king's
hand. I believe you may have a lodging near
me.—I am, etc., CHARLES MONTAGUE."

It should be understood that in this office
Newton had an opportunity of serving his country, by the application of his scientific knowledge to the new coinage. The work was soon
afterwards completed. During the four years
in which he held this appointment, he retained
his mathematical chair in Cambridge; but
when he was promoted to the mastership of the
Mint, worth twelve or fifteen hundred pounds
a year, he resigned his chair to Mr. Whiston.

Newton now took his appropriate place among
the great public men of Europe. He was one
of the few foreign associates of the Royal
Academy of Sciences at Paris. Two years
later, he was re-elected to represent the university of Cambridge in parliament; and, in 1703,
he became president of the Royal Society of
London, an office to which he was re-appointed
every year until his death. The honour of

knighthood was conferred on him by queen Anne, on her royal visit to Cambridge, in 1705. In 1709, a second edition of the " Principia" was sent out from the university press of Cambridge. Dr. Bentley prevailed on Roger Cotes, Plumian professor of astronomy at Cambridge, to superintend its publication. The correspondence between Mr. Cotes and sir Isaac Newton, in relation to the improvements of this edition, has recently been published, in the work which has been quoted, by Mr. Edleston, fellow of Trinity College. Some extracts from the letters are here given. The first is a letter from Dr. Bentley, saying : " I waited to-day on sir Isaac Newton, who will be glad to see you in town here, and then put into your hands one part of his book, corrected for ye press." Sir Isaac kept back the corrected copy for some weeks, when Cotes thus addressed him :—

"Cambridge, August 18, 1709.

" Sir,—The earnest desire I have to see a new edition of y^r *Princip.* makes me somewhat impatient 'till we receive y^r copy of it, which you was pleased to promise me about the middle of the last month you would send down in about a fortnight's time. I hope you will pardon me for this uneasiness, from which I cannot free myself, and for giving you this trouble to

let you know it. I have been so much obliged
to you, by yourself and by y^r book, y^t (I desire
you to believe me) I think myself bound in
gratitude to take all the care I possibly can that
it shall be correct. Some days ago I was
examining," etc.

In October, he received the following answer
from sir Isaac :—

" Sir,—I sent you, by Mr. Whiston, the
greatest part of ye copy of my ' Principia,' in
order to a new edition. I then forgot to correct
an error in the first sheet. I thank you for
your letter, and the corrections of the two
theorems in ye Treatise de Quadratura. I would
not have you be at the trouble of examining
all the Demonstrations in the ' Principia.' It's
impossible to print the book without some
faults, and if you print by the copy sent you,
correcting only such faults as occur in reading
over the sheets to correct them as they are
printed off, you will have labour more than it's
fit to give you.

" Mr. Livebody is a composer, (I mean Mr.
Livebody who made the wooden cutts,) and he
thinks he can sett the cutts better than other
composers can, and offers to come down to Cambridge and assist in composing, if it be thought
fit. When you have printed off one or two

sheets, if you please to send me a copy of them,
I will send you a further supply of wooden
cutts.

" I am, your most humble and faithful
servant, Is. NEWTON."

The correspondence, of which this is a part,
took place during the excitement produced by
the preaching and the trial of Sacheverell, and
also at the period of Marlborough's exploits in
the war with France.   The next letter, from
Cotes to Newton, and, indeed, nearly all that
follow, are intelligible to mathematicians only,
and to such as take an interest in minute and
exact experiments in natural philosophy.   To
the general reader, however, it is interesting to
know with what pains and labour this eminent
philosopher attended to the smallest particulars
connected with his great work, and with what
calmness, courtesy, and even gratitude, he
accepted or discussed the objections and suggestions of Cotes.   The interruptions and delays,
frequently referred to in the correspondence,
were occasioned by sir Isaac's engagements at
the Mint and at the Royal Society.   Still, he
was intent on the correct appearance of his
"Principia," and was almost daily writing about
it.   The number of the emendations, involving
a vast number of figures and calculations, is

such as to surprise even those who are accustomed to such matters. In a letter to Dr. Bentley about the preface, Mr. Cotes says : " I should be glad to know from sir Isaac with what view he thinks proper to have it written. You know the book has been received abroad with some disadvantage, and the cause it may be easily guessed at. The ' *Commercium Epistolicum*,' lately published by order of the Royal Society, gives such indubitable proof of Mr. Leibnitz's want of candour, that I shall not scruple in the least to speak out the full truth of the matter, if it be thought convenient. There are some pieces of his looking this way which deserve a censure, as his ' *Tentamen de Motuum Cœlestium Causis*.' If sir Isaac is willing that something of this nature may be done, I should be glad if, whilst I am making the index, he would be pleased to consider of it, and put down a few notes of what he thinks most material to be insisted on. This I say upon supposition that I write the preface myself. But I think it will be much more advisable that YOU or HE or both of YOU should write it whilst you are in town. You may depend upon it that I will own it and defend it as well as I can, if hereafter there be occasion." Dr. Bentley's reply is subjoined :

"At sir Isaac Newton's, March 12.

" Dear sir,—I communicated your letter to sir Isaac, who happened to make me a visit this morning, and we appointed to meet this evening at his house, and there to write you an answer. For the close of your letter, which proposes a preface to be drawn up here, and to be fathered by you, we will impute it to your modesty ; but you must not press it further, but go about it yourself. For the subject of your preface, you know it must be—to give an account, first, of the work itself ; secondly, of the improvements of the new edition ; and then you have sir Isaac's consent to add what you think proper about the controversy of the first invention. You yourself are full master of it, and want no hints to be given you ; however, when it is drawn up, you have his and my judgment, to suggest anything that may improve it. 'Tis both our opinions to spare the *name* of M. Leibnitz, and abstain from all words and epithets of repro(a)ch ; for else that will be the reply, (not that it is untrue,) but that it is rude and uncivil. Sir Isaac presents his service to you."

The letter in which Cotes acknowledged Dr. Bentley's reply contains so full a sketch of the actual contents of the "Principia" that we here transcribe it :—

"Sir,—I have received Dr. Bentley's letter in answer to that I wrote him concerning the preface. I am very well satisfied with the directions there given, and have accordingly been considering of the matter. I think it will be proper, besides the account of the book and its improvements, to add something more particularly concerning the manner of philosophizing made use of, and wherein it differs from that of Des Cartes and others ; I mean, in *first demonstrating the* PRINCIPLE *it employs.* This I would not only assert, but make evident by a short deduction of the *principle of gravity* from the phenomena of nature, in a popular way, that it may be understood by ordinary readers, and may serve, at the same time, as a specimen to them of the method of the whole book. That you (may) the better understand what I aim at, I think to proceed in some such manner. 'Tis one of the primary laws of nature that all bodies persevere in their state, etc. Hence it follows that bodies which are moved in curve lines, and continually hindered from going on along the tangents to close curve lines, must be acted upon by some force sufficient for that purpose. The planets ('tis matter of fact) revolve in curve lines, therefore, etc. Again, 'tis mathematically demonstrated, that *every*

body which is moved, etc. Now 'tis confessed by
all astronomers that the primary planets about
the sun, and the secondary about their respective
primaries, do describe areas proportional to the
times. Therefore, the force by which they are
continually diverted from the tangents of their
orbits (from going on in a strait lyne) is directed
and tends towards their central bodies ; which
force (from what cause soever it proceeds) may
therefore not improperly be called *centripetal*,
in respect of the revolving bodies, and *attractive*
in respect of the central ones. Furthermore,
'tis mathematically demonstrated, that cor. 6,
prop. 4, lib. 1, and cor. 1, prop. 45, lib. 1. But
'tis agreed upon by astronomers that, etc., etc.
Therefore, the centripetal forces of the primary
planets revolving about the sun, and of the
secondary planets revolving about their primary
ones, are in a duplicate proportion, etc. In this
manner I would proceed to the 4th prop. of lib.
3, and then to the 5th. . . . . After this specimen, I think it will be proper to add some
things by which your book may be cleared from
some prejudices which have been industriously
laid against it ; as that it deserts mechanical
causes, is built upon miracles, and recurs to
occult qualities. That you may not think it
unnecessary to answer such objections, you may

be pleased to consult a weekly paper called *Memoires of Literature*, and sold by Ann Baldwin, in Warwick Lane.   In the eighteenth number of the second volume of those papers, which was published May 5th, 1712,* you will find a very extraordinary letter of M. Leibnitz to Mr. Hartsoeker, which will confirm what I have said.   I do not propose to mention M. Leibnitz's name ; 'twere best to neglect *him;* but the *objections,* I think, may very well be answered, and even retorted upon the maintainers of vortices.   After I have spoke of your book, it will come in my way to mention the improvements of geometry upon which your book is built, and there I must mention the time when those improvements were first made, and by whom they were made.   I intend to say nothing of M. Leibnitz, but desire you will give me leave to appeal to the ' *Commercium Epistolicum,*' and vouch what I shall say of yourself, and to insert in my preface the very words of the judgment of the Society, that foreigners may more generally be acquainted with the true state of the case."

In reply to this letter, Newton suggests vari-

---

* P. 137. Leibnitz, opp. tom. iii. pars, 2, p. 60. This letter is dated Hanover, Feb. 10, 1711. Leibnitz does not mention Newton's name.

ous improvements in the work, and says, " If you write any further preface I must not see it, for I find that I shall be examined about it." The preface actually prefixed to the new edition of the " Principia" was different from the one proposed in the letter to Newton ; it contained no " account of the book," but, instead of that, the indices, drawn up by Cotes, who also prepared an exposition of the manner of philosophizing made use of, an examination of the objections of Leibnitz, but without naming that philosopher, and a criticism on the Cartesian theory of vortices.

The new edition was published in 1713. On the 27th of July, Newton had the honour of waiting on the queen, to present a copy to her majesty. The extreme accuracy with which the author and his friends revised this great work appears from the correspondence of Newton with Cotes, recently published, and previously referred to by us. In the same volume, the correspondence of Newton with Keil, and a large body of notes, will serve more fully to elucidate the controversy which has been adverted to between Newton and Leibnitz. There is a curious letter in this volume respecting Mr. Whiston, who had been expelled from the university of Cambridge as an obstinate heretic. It is from Cotes to John Smith :—

" Sir,—I thank God we go on very well. I hope you are all in good health, notwithstanding this very sickly season. I suppose my cousin told you in his letter which he wrote on Tuesday last, that he has received the £10 which you sent him. I talked with Mr. Whiston today, and gave him your advice of making a recantation, for which he thanks you, but will not accept it. I have been long ago well satisfied that no advice from any private person can possibly have any effect upon him. I asked him, therefore, whether the judgment of the convocation might not be a sufficient ground for him to alter his opinions, and whether he should not think himself obliged to desist, if he should chance to be censured by them ; he answered me in the negative, unless they would prove to him that his opinions were wrong. I afterwards told him, that the church must, in three or four years, recover its primitive purity, according to his own exposition of the Revelations, and that, therefore, it would be, perhaps, advisable for him to stay till that time, and expect the issue with patience. Upon this he could not help discovering himself, (as I imagined he would do,) and told me that the completion of that prophecy might, he believed, depend in a good measure upon the reviving of those ancient doctrines in which he was at present engaged.   He bid me consider what answer St. Paul would have given to one that should have dissuaded him from preaching the gospel upon this reason—that it was certainly foretold that the gospel should be preached to all nations. You may easily understand by these answers upon what grounds he is so very resolute.   I am persuaded 'tis in vain to endeavour to reclaim him till the term of that prophecy be expired."

A copy of the "Principia" having been presented by Cotes to sir William Jones, it was acknowledged in the following terms :—

" 'Tis impossible to represent to you with what pleasure I received your inestimable present of the ' Principia,' and am much concerned to find myself so deeply charged with obligations to you, and such, I fear, as all my future endeavours will never be able to requite.   This edition is, indeed, exceeding beautiful, and interspersed with great variety of admirable discoveries, so very natural to its great author; but is much more so from the additional advantage of your excellent preface, prefixed, which I wish might be got published in some of the foreign journals; and, since a better account of this book cannot be given, I suppose it will not be difficult to get it done."

It may not be amiss to mention here, that Voltaire found many objections, in Paris, to the discoveries of Newton. He studied the system for some weeks under S'Gravesande, at Leyden, and published the " Elements of the Philosophy of Newton," at Amsterdam. While on a visit at Paris, he wrote a letter to professor Smith, of Cambridge, with whom, it is probable, he had become acquainted while residing in this country twelve years before. The letter is short, and is inserted in this place because of its reference to Newton:—

" Sir,—I have perused your book of 'Optics.' I cannot be so mightily pleased with a book without loving the author. Give me leave to submit to your judgement these little answers of mine, which I have writt against some ignorant ennemies of sir Isaac Newton, whom you follow so closely in the path of truth and glory. —I am, sir, your most humble, obed. servant,

" VOLTAIRE."

The high standing of sir Isaac Newton, as a public man, a philosopher, and a professor of Christianity, drew towards him the attention of the princess of Wales, who became afterwards queen-consort to king George II.

With Leibnitz, who was an inhabitant of the
city of Hanover, and a councillor of the elector,
she maintained a learned correspondence. That
eminent philosopher had carried his opposition
to Newton so far as to represent to the princess
that the Newtonian philosophy was both false
as a physical system, and hostile to religion.
The princess had cherished the society and
benefited by the conversation of the English
philosopher, and she was known to express her
admiration of his genius in the most open
manner. The attempt of Leibnitz to injure
the reputation of Newton was not unknown to
the king. His majesty intimated a wish that
Newton should answer the imputations of the
Hanoverian philosopher. The answer, which
was read by the princess, appears to have been
satisfactory to the court, for sir Isaac continued
to enjoy the royal favour.

In one of Newton's conversations with the
princess, some portions of ancient history induced him to mention a new system of chronology which he had drawn up, as a refreshment
when weary with severer studies at Cambridge.
The princess, some time after, received a copy
of this system for her own personal use, not to
be shown to any other person. At the request
of her royal highness, sir Isaac permitted the

abbé Conté to have a copy of this manuscript,
on the same condition of keeping it secret.   It
was a short chronicle, from the first memory of
things in Europe to the conquest of Persia by
Alexander the Great.   As soon as the abbé
went to France, he showed it to M. Freret, an
antiquary in Paris, who translated it into
French, and published it, with observations of
his own against its principles.   This publication, to which the author had refused his consent, drew from sir Isaac some remarks, which
were printed in the thirty-fourth volume of
the Transactions of the Royal Society.   Besides
blaming both the abbé and the publisher, he
showed that the annotator had mistaken the
contents of the paper.   Another French writer,
father Souciet, published no less than five
dissertations on the new chronology.   Sir Isaac
was persuaded by his friends to prepare for the
press his celebrated work on chronology, which,
however, was not published until after his
decease.   This work was entitled, " The Chronology of several Kingdoms amended; to which
is prefixed a Short Chronicle, from the first
memory of things in Europe to the conquest of
Persia by Alexander the Great," and dedicated
by Mr. Conduit to the queen.   It is divided
into six chapters: the first, treating of the

chronology of the Greeks ; the second, of the
empire of Egypt ; the third, of the Assyrian
empire ; the fourth, of the two contemporary
empires of the Babylonians and the Medes;
the fifth, of the Temple of Solomon; and the
last, of the empire of the Persians.   We are
told, in the Life of Whiston, that sir Isaac
wrote with his own hand not fewer than eighteen
copies of the chapter on the Grecian chronology.   In the thirty-fourth and thirty-fifth
volumes of the Philosophical Transactions, Dr.
Halley replied to the astronomical dissertations
of Souciet against the chronology of Newton.
His views were opposed also by several
writers both in England and in France, but
they were supported by others.   A history
of the controversy is given by M. Daunou, in
a note to M. Biot's Life of Newton in the
" *Biographie Universelle*."   That able and ingenious writer regards " the system of Newton
as a great fact in the history of chronological
science, and as confirming the observation of
Varro—that the stage of history does not com-
mence till the first Olympiad."   Of course, this
observation on *general* history leaves untouched
the particular narratives of the ancient Hebrew
Scriptures, which received the sanction of
the Son of God, were referred to as authentic

and Divine by inspired apostles, and are continually receiving fresh illustrations from discoveries in the antiquities of Egypt and of Assyria.

In the Gentleman's Magazine for 1755 there is a "Letter to a Person of Distinction," who had desired the writer's opinion on a hypothesis which had been offered by bishop Lloyd on the form of the most ancient year. The letter, which is without date, had been sent to Dr. Prideaux, author of the "Connexion between Sacred and Profane History," by the bishop of Worcester. It is given as the production of sir Isaac, and it bears internal marks of genuineness. He speaks well of the ingenuity of the hypothesis, but concludes, from an examination of the years mentioned by all ancient nations, that they did not use the year of twelve months, or 360 days, according to the opinion of bishop Lloyd, but either the luni-solar, or lunar, or solar, or the calendar of these years. A year of 360 days is not any of them. "The beginning of such a year," he says, "would have run round the four seasons in seventy years; and such a notable fact would have been mentioned in history, and is not to be asserted without proving it."

CHAPTER VI.

Newton's chemical studies—Heat—Fire—Flame—Elective
attraction—Structure of bodies—Ether—Electricity—
Inventions—Experiments with the retina.

FROM his earliest years at school, Newton's mind
had been more or less engaged in chemical
studies. He was led to the further prosecution
of them by his anxiety to know the best materials for the specula of reflecting telescopes;
and to his active mind everything connected
with the correct apprehension of the works of
God presented objects of attraction, and, we
may hope, aids to intelligent devotion. He
communicated several valuable papers on
chemical subjects to the Royal Society, and
they are frequently referred to in his correspondence with Oldenburg, the secretary of the
society. From these papers, we gather the
views of this cautious philosopher on many of
the interesting questions which have so successfully engaged the attention of the great writers
on scientific chemistry.

By a series of careful experiments, he formed a scale of the gradations of heat, from the freezing point of water to the heat of a small coal fire, in which he shows that equal parts of tin and bismuth melt at a degree of heat four times greater than blood heat, and lead at a degree of heat twice as great as that which melts the tin and bismuth, while the heat of a small coal fire is twice as great as that at which lead is melted.

By using a thermometer of linseed oil, he ascertained that the oil was rarefied by the heat of the human body in the proportion of 40 to 39 ; by the heat of boiling water in the proportion of 15 to 14 ; by the heat of melting tin, beginning to solidify, in the proportion of 15 to 13 ; and by the heat of the same tin, when it has reached the solid state, in the proportion of 28 to 20. He found the rarefaction of oil to be *fifteen times* greater than that of spirits of wine, and the rarefaction of air to be *ten* times greater than that of oil. The rarefaction was proportioned to the degree of heat.

In a paper, written after the " Principia," " *De Natura Acidorum*," (On the Nature of Acids,) he put forth his opinions on fire, flame, and electric attractions. Fire is a body so heated as to emit light copiously. Flame is a

vapour heated so hot as to shine. The small
particles of bodies act on each other at distances
too minute to be detected by observation. By
these attractive forces he explains the spon-
taneous melting of salt of tartar in the atmo-
sphere ; the necessity of great heat to distil
water from salt of tartar ; the tenacity with
which sulphuric acid combines with water ;
the production of flame from cold fluids ; ful-
minating powders, and many other chemical
affinities ; hot springs ; volcanoes ; fire-damp ;
the glittering appearance of several minerals ;
cohesion ; capillary attraction ; earthquakes ;
thunder and lightning ; hurricanes ; water-
spouts; and landslips. On the same principle
of elective attraction, he explains the varieties
in the structure of hard, elastic, malleable, soft,
fluid, and humid bodies, and the round figure
of drops of fluid and of the globe.

There is a curious tract in the works of
William Law, author of the "Serious Call," in
which he speaks of sir Isaac Newton as a dili-
gent student of the alchymical writings of
Jacob Boehm. "That in the early part of his
life he had paid some attention to studies of
this nature would appear from many papers
in the Portsmouth Collection, in sir Isaac's
own writing, of Flammel's Explication of

Hieroglyphic Figures; and in another hand, many sheets of William Yworth's *Processus Mysterii Magni Philosophicus;* and also from the manner in which sir Isaac requests Mr. Aston to inquire after one Borry in Holland, who always went clothed in green, and who was said to possess valuable secrets; but Mr. Law has weakened the force of his own testimony, when he asserts that Newton borrowed the doctrine of attraction from Boehm's three first propositions of eternal nature."[*]

The first appearance of Newton's opinions respecting ether, and its connexion with light and with gravitation, was in a paper containing *"An hypothesis explaining properties of light."* The word *ether* was used by the Ionian philosophers to describe the space, or that which occupies the space, between the heavenly bodies. By modern philosophers ether is a term used in a somewhat different application, and is explained by Humboldt in the first part of the third volume of his " Cosmos." At one time, Newton had indulged in some " guesses," as he calls them in a letter to Dr. Halley, respecting ether, as explaining many phenomena in nature. We find that he afterwards abandoned them; but they subsequently re-

* Brewster's Life of Newton, p. 303.

appeared in the second English edition of his
"Optics." In the queries appended to that work,
he speaks of a medium more subtile than air
by means of which heat is transmitted, and light
reflected and refracted, pervading all bodies,
and spread through the heavens, varying in
density, and producing the effect which we call
gravity. The undulatory theory of light regards
light as the impression made on the eye by the
undulations or wave-like motion of this ethereal
medium. Newton, on the contrary, regarded
light as a substance *radiating* from luminous
bodies with great velocity in all directions.
These rays, or continuous particles of light, he
supposed to pass *through* the ether, and, by thus
passing through it, causing pulsations in the
ether, by which their own velocity is speeded
or checked, thus falling into those "*fits*" which
he so often mentions, of "easy transmission."
Thus he accounts for the *refraction* of light,
and the functions of vision and of hearing,
"and he is of opinion that animal motion may
be performed by the vibrations of the same
medium, excited in the brain by the power of the
will, and propagated from thence by the solid,
pellucid, and uniform capillamenta of the nerves
into the muscles for contracting and dilating
them." Some interesting experiments were

made by sir Isaac in exciting electricity by friction on glass. He invented the instrument well known to navigators as "Hadley's Quadrant," several years before its production by Mr. Hadley. He also invented an improved microscope, which has since been carried to a higher degree of perfection by M. Amici; and he suggested an improvement of a somewhat different kind, which was realized long after by sir David Brewster. Among the inventions of sir Isaac we may mention that of the Prismatic Reflector, by means of which the use of a single glass secures the erection of the object, and varies the magnifying power of the telescope, by altering the distances between the speculum, the prism, and the eye-glass.

In Newton's correspondence with Locke, the latter had mentioned to him some observations which occurred in Mr. Boyle's book respecting colours. Sir Isaac, in his reply, says that he had made a similar observation upon himself, with the hazard of his eyes. "The manner was this: I looked a very little while upon the sun in the looking-glass with my left eye, and then turned my eyes into a dark corner of my chamber, and winked, to observe the impression made, and the circles of colours which encompassed it, and how they decayed by degrees, and at last vanished. This I repeated a second and a third time. At the third time, when the phantasm of light and colours were almost vanished, intending my fancy upon them to see their last appearance, I found, to my amazement, that they began to return, and, by little and little, to become as lively and vivid as when I had newly looked upon the sun. But, when I ceased to intend my fancy upon them they vanished again. After this, I found that as often as I went into the dark, and intended my mind upon them, as when a man looks earnestly to see anything which is difficult to be seen, I could make the phantasm return without looking any more upon the sun; and the oftener I made it return, the more easily I could make it return again, and at length by repeating this without looking any more upon the sun, I made such an impression on my eye, that if I looked upon the clouds, or a book, or any bright object, I saw upon it a round bright spot of light like the sun; and, which is still stranger, though I looked upon the sun with my right eye only, and not with my left, yet the fancy began to make the impression upon my left eye as well as upon my right—for if I shut my right eye, and looked upon a book or the clouds with my left eye, I could see the spectrum of

the sun almost as plain as with my right eye, if
I did but intend my fancy a little while upon it ;
for at first, if I shut my right eye, and looked
with my left, the spectrum of the sun did not
appear till I intended my fancy upon it ; but
by repeating, this appeared every time more
easily ; and now, in a few hours' time, I had
brought my eyes to such a pass, that I could
look upon no bright object with either eye but
I saw the sun before me, so that I durst neither
write nor read ; but to recover the use of my
eyes, shut myself up in a chamber made dark
for three days together, and used all means to
divert my imagination from the sun ; for if I
thought upon him, I presently saw his picture,
though I was in the dark. But, by keeping in
the dark, and employing my mind about other
things, I began in three or four days to have
the use of my eyes again ; and by forbearing a
few days longer to look upon bright objects,
recovered them pretty well, though not so
well but that for some months after the spectrum of the sun began to return as often as I
began to meditate upon the phenomenon, even
though I lay in bed at midnight with my cur-
tains drawn ; but now I have been very well
for many years, though I am apt to think that
if I durst venture my eyes, I could still make

the phantasm return by the power of my fancy. This story I tell you, to let you understand, that in the observation related by Mr. Boyle, the man's fancy probably concurred with the impression made by the sun's light, to produce that phantasm of the sun which he constantly saw in bright objects; and so your question about the cause of this phantasm involves another about the power of fancy, which I confess is too hard a knot for me to untie. To place this effect on a constant motion is hard, because the sun ought then to appear perpetually. It seems rather to consist in a disposition of the sensorium to move the imagination strongly, and to be easily moved by the imagination and by the light, as often as bright objects are looked upon."

It is not a little remarkable, that long before the observations of sir Isaac Newton, so minutely reported in the preceding extract, were given to the world, sir David Brewster had described similar phenomena in the Edinburgh Encyclopædia.

CHAPTER VII.

IN referring to the theological views of so eminent a philosopher, it is important to observe, that the doctrines of the gospel are *the same to the philosopher as to the simplest peasant*, who diligently reads the Scriptures, or attentively hears the preaching of their truths. The truths of natural science are built on facts, ascertained by observation, tested by experiment, and supported by reasoning. The truths of the gospel *are* facts. That man is fallen, guilty, depraved, and wretched, is *one* fact, or collection of facts. That the Son of God became man, in order to obey the law which we have broken, and to bear the curse which we deserve, is *another* fact, or series of facts. That the Holy Spirit is given to renew sinful men after the image of God, to guide them to the Saviour, to enlighten, purify, and console those who, through grace, believe the gospel, is likewise a *fact*, or, rather, the brief statement of many facts. The revealed *mode of viewing* these facts, imparted by inspired teachers, constitutes the *doctrines* of the gospel. To understand these sacred truths, so as to be saved through believing them, men need not a capacious intellect, a disciplined mind, or great stores of what the world calls learning, but a heart so humbled by the Spirit of God as to receive them, on HIS TESTIMONY, in the "love of the truth." Whether such was the experience of our great English philosopher we have now no means of knowing, and it is no part of our business to conjecture. It should be remembered that, in his days, there was comparatively little evangelical life and earnestness in the public teaching of any of the British churches; and also, that a mind so cautious, so humble, so trained to rigid evidence, as that of Newton, was not likely, especially in that age, to communicate freely its private experiences in connexion with the gospel. To an enlightened believer it is of no moment—as to his own faith—whether others have believed or not; his faith stands, "not in the wisdom of men, but in the power of God." It would, indeed, be most interesting to know more than we can now know of the spiritual history of the most highly gifted of mankind in the department of natural philosophy ; but, in the absence of such knowledge, we can but express the hope that he, whose belief in God was so sublime, whose reverence for Scripture was so profound, whose observance of the religious institutions of his church was so irreproachable—was not a man to stop short in theories and in forms, but to pass beyond them to the Divine light, the holy enjoyments, and the blessed hopes of the spiritual church of the living God.

If it should be that such a hope is not well-founded, then, indeed, there would be a serious and remarkable illustration of all those words of Jesus and of his apostles, in which we are taught that it is not human wisdom, but Divine illumination, that leads men to the knowledge of themselves as offenders against the supreme law, and to trust in that Divine Saviour, by whom alone they can worship God acceptably. But if, on the contrary, we are right in our hope of meeting this great expounder of the law of the material creation among the redeemed and sanctified followers of Him who gave, who expounded, who vindicated, who fulfilled, who magnified and honoured the higher law of the spiritual creation—then shall we behold a glorious confirmation of the truth, that the highest order of intellect, and the highest treasures of knowledge, are not incompatible with humble penitence, with grateful faith, and with the meekness of a servant of Jesus. There is abundant proof that Newton was a professed believer of the gospel from his early years, that he was learned in the Scriptures, and that it was his familiar habit, his chosen occupation, to be much engaged in the reading of religious books. In the prime of life, he was much employed in the profound study of Biblical subjects. To him the Bible was, in spiritual things, what the visible heavens and earth were in natural things—the witness for God, the manifestation of his wisdom, the display of his power, the assertion of his righteous government, and the revelation of his saving grace. With the same humbleness of mind with which he laid aside the opinions of speculative philosophy, that he might observe the works of God as He had made them, and sustained them, and, by means of them, declared himself to man, and accomplished his benevolent designs—Newton came to the study of the Scriptures, bent on knowing what they *are*, what they *contain*, what they *mean*, and with *what purposes* the holy men of God were moved by the Spirit to write them for the instruction of mankind. It has never been alleged that Newton was an atheist, or an infidel; though it has been insinuated that he rejected the sublime doctrine of the oneness of the Father, and the Son, and the Holy Ghost, in the mystery of God. For this insinuation we find *no warrant* in any portion of his writings, or in any act of his life. On the contrary, we find him referring to this doctrine as " the faith " of the church of Christ in all ages ; and he indignantly resented the conduct of Whiston, in reporting him to be an Arian.

This is not the place for giving a complete account of the theological writings of Newton; yet, even in so brief a biography, we cannot entirely pass them by. His correspondence with Locke, and Bentley, and other contemporaries, contains frequent intimations of the interest which he cherished in these sacred studies.

His first letter to Locke refers to some papers which he had written concerning the critical history of two passages in the New Testament. In a second letter, he says, "I hope we shall meet again in due time, and then I should be glad to have your judgment upon some of my mystical fancies. The Son of Man, Dan. vii., I take to be the same with the Word of God upon the white horse in heaven, at Rev. xix., and him to be the same with the Man Child, Rev. xii., for both are to rule the nations with a rod of iron; but whence are you certain that 'the Ancient of Days' is Christ? Does Christ anywhere sit upon the throne? Know you the meaning of Dan. x. 21, *'There is none that holdeth with me in these things, but Michael your prince?'*" Again, in a third letter to Locke, he says: " Concerning ' the Ancient of Days,' Dan. vii., there seems to be a mistake either in my last letter or in yours, because you wrote in your former letter that 'the Ancient of Days' is Christ; and in my last, I either did, or should have asked, how you knew that. But these discourses may be done with more freedom at our next meeting." In another letter to the same correspondent, he makes an observation which, though we do not concur in it, shows that he had a reverential regard for the testimonies of ancient churches, while he uses his characteristic caution in offering a positive opinion on a subject which is worthy of severe examination. " Miracles of good credit continued in the church for about two or three hundred years. Gregory Thauma-turgus (wonder-worker) had his name from thence, and was one of the latest who was

eminent for that gift ; but of their number and
frequency I am not able to give you a just
account. The *history of these ages is very
imperfect.*"

From a fourth letter to Locke, the following
extracts show with what accurate patience he
was studying the questions that arose between
several parties of divines. " Concerning mira-
cles, there is a notable passage or two in
Irenæus, l. 22, c. 56, recited by Eusebius,
l. 5, c. 17. The miraculous refection of the
Roman army by rain, at the prayers of a
Christian legion, (thence called *fulminatrix*,
thundering,) is mentioned by Ziphilina apud
Drogen, in Marco Imp., and by Tertullian,
(Apol. c. 5, and ad Scap. c. 4 ;) and by
Eusebius, l. 5, c. 5, Hist. Eccl. ; and in
Chronico ;) and acknowledged by the emperor
Marcus in a letter, as Tertullian mentions.
The same Tertullian somewhere challenges the
heathens to produce a demoniac, and he will
produce a man who shall cast out the demon ;
for this was the language of the ancients for
curing lunatics. I am told that sir Henry
Yelveston, in a book about the truth of Chris-
tianity, has writ well of the ancient miracles,
but the book I never saw. Concerning Gregory
Thaumaturgus, see Gregory Nyssa in ' *ejus vita*,'

(his life;) and Basil, '*De Spiritu Sancto*,' c. 29."

The whole of the following letter will be read with interest, as addressed by Newton to Locke, whatever judgment the reader may form of the explanation which it gives of the passage of Scripture to which it relates. That Locke himself did not adopt it, appears from his paraphrasing the words in the printed copy of his work, "the unbelieving husband is sanctified, or made a Christian, by his wife."

"London, May 15, 1703

" Sir,—Upon my first receiving your papers, I read over those concerning the first Epistle to the Corinthians; but by so many intermissions that I resolved to go over them again, so soon as I could get leisure to do it with more attention. I have now read it over a second time, and gone over also your papers on the second Epistle. Some faults, which seemed to be faults of the scribe, I mended with my pen, as I read the papers; some others I have noted in the inclosed papers. In your paraphrase on 1 Cor. vii. 14, you say, ' The unbelieving husband is sanctified, or made a Christian, by his wife.' I doubt this interpretation, because the unbelieving husband is not capable of baptism, as all Christians are. The Jews looked upon themselves as clean, holy, or separate to God, and other nations as unclean, unholy, or common ; and, accordingly, it was unlawful 'for a man that was a Jew to keep company with, or come unto one of another nation,' Acts x. 28. But when the propagation of the gospel made it necessary for the Jews who preached the gospel to go unto and keep company with the Gentiles, God showed Peter by a vision, in the case of Cornelius, that he had cleansed those of other nations, so that Peter should not any longer call any man common or unclean, and on that account forbear their company ; and thereupon Peter went in unto Cornelius and his companions, who were uncircumcised, and did eat with them, Acts x. 27, 28, and xi. 3. Sanctifying, therefore, and cleansing, signify here, not the making a man a Jew or Christian, but the dispensing with the law whereby the people of God were to avoid the company of the rest of the world as unholy or unclean. And if this sense be applied to St. Paul's words, they will signify, that, although believers are a people holy to God, and ought to avoid the company of unbelievers as unholy or unclean, yet this law is dispensed with in some cases, and particularly in the case of marriage, (by parties before the conversion of either the husband or the wife.) The believing wife must not separate from the unbelieving husband, as unholy or unclean, nor the believing husband from the unbelieving wife; for the unbeliever is sanctified or cleansed by marriage with the believer, the law of avoiding the company of unbelievers being in this case dispensed with. I should, therefore, interpret St. Paul's words after the following manner:—'For the unbelieving husband is sanctified or cleansed by the believing wife, so that it is lawful to keep him company, and the unbelieving wife is sanctified by the husband; else were the children of such parents to be separated from you, and avoided as unclean; but now, by nursing and educating them in your families, you allow that they are holy.' This interpretation I propose as easy and suiting well to the words and design of St. Paul, but submit it wholly to your judgment. I think your paraphrase and commentary on these two Epistles is done with very great care and judgment."

Dr. Bentley, who had been appointed to preach the first course of sermons on Boyle's Lecture, devoted the seventh and eighth sermons of his course to the proof of Divine Providence founded on the physical constitution of the universe, as demonstrated in Newton's "Principia." While he was preparing these discourses, he

encountered the argument of Lucretius that
the world had existed from eternity, the
matter of which it consists being equally
diffused, and possessing an innate power of
gravity. He had previously studied a series of
works recommended to him by Newton, and had
made himself master of the "Principia." He
now addressed some queries to the philosopher
on the difficulty before him. In answer to these
queries, Newton wrote his "Four Letters addressed to Dr. Bentley, containing some arguments in proof of a Deity." In these letters he
informs Bentley, that in the third book of the
"Principia" he had a view to such principles as
might lead considering men "to the belief of a
Deity." He shows that natural causes cannot
explain how matter should be divided into
shining and opaque bodies; that no reason can
be discovered why one body should be fitted to
give light and heat to all the rest, but the will
of the presiding Mind; that the movements of
the planetary system were so adjusted as to
exhibit a Being well skilled in mechanics and
geometry; that only a Divine Intelligence could
have given the planets the quantity of power,
as well as the kind of motion, with which they
revolve round the sun as their centre; and that
a supernatural power alone can account for the

existence and the arrangements of the material universe.

The principal theological work of sir Isaac Newton is his "Observations on the Prophecies of Daniel and the Apocalypse of St. John." In the first part, on the prophecies of Daniel, he gives a brief account of the Old Testament writings, especially of the book of Daniel, and the place which it occupies among the prophetical books. He then explains the figurative language of the prophets. Having done this, he applies the explanations to the great image of gold, silver, brass, and iron, as representing the empire of the Babylonians, the Persians, the Greeks, and the Romans, while "the stone cut out of the mountain without hands" represents a new kingdom, which was to arise after the other four, to conquer all nations, and last till the end of time. He explains the vision of the four beasts as representing the same four kingdoms under another aspect, and with larger intimations. The united kingdom of Babylon and Media, by which the Assyrian power was subdued, was represented by a lion with eagle's wings. The Persian empire, together with the kingdoms of Sardis, Babylon, and Egypt, was represented by a bear with "three ribs in the mouth of it, within the teeth of it." The Greek

empire, with the kingdoms of Cassander, Lysi-
machus, Ptolemy, Seleucus, was represented by
a leopard, with four heads and four wings.   The
Roman empire, and the ten separate kingdoms
into which it was broken up in the reign of
Theodosius the Great, was represented by the
" fourth beast, dreadful and terrible, and strong
exceedingly," with great iron teeth and ten
horns.   The church of Rome — as a seer, a
prophet, and a king—is represented by the
" little horn," which came up among the other
horns, " before whom there were three of the
first horns plucked up by the roots," and in
which were " eyes like the eyes of a man, and a
mouth speaking great things."   The kingdom
of the Medes and Persians, from the beginning
of the four empires, was represented by *the
ram and the he-goat.*   The kingdom of the
Greeks, to the *end* of the four empires, was represented by the he-goat.   The last prophecy of
Daniel, sir Isaac regarded as a commentary on
the previous vision of the ram and the he-goat ;
and he understands the prophecy of the king
" doing according to his will, magnifying himself above every God, honouring ' Mahuzzim,'
and not regarding the desire of women," as
representing the Greek or Eastern empire, after
its separation from the Western or Latin empire.

The remarkable prophecy of the Seventy Weeks is explained as fulfilled in the *times* of the Messiah's first coming, and also of his second coming.

In that part of the work which treats of the Apocalypse, he expresses his opinion that this book was written at an earlier period than the Epistles of Peter and the Epistle to the Hebrews ; and, having explained the scenery of the visions in relation to the temple-worship at Jerusalem, he traces the connexion of the Apocalypse with the book of Daniel, and then proceeds to illustrate his views of this closing prophecy. On all these prophecies he makes the judicious and valuable observation, that they were not given to gratify our curiosity about the future, but to afford convincing proofs that the world is governed by Providence ; and he declares that his own design is to follow in the steps of previous writers, of whom, he says, " there is scarce one of note who hath not made some discovery worth knowing."

In reviewing thus briefly the theological writings of sir Isaac Newton, we are naturally led to observe, that none of them relate to the peculiar truths of the gospel, but belong to departments of study, which, when kept in their own place, as preparatory and auxiliary to the gospel itself, are of exceedingly great

value.   In the present day especially, when
vigorous and persevering efforts are made to
undermine the faith which Christians hold—
by superstition, on the one hand, and by speculative infidelity, in the garb of learning, science,
and philosophy, on the other—it is of no small
importance that we should be on our guard
against both these evils.   Assuming, as we
believe, on the most solid and well-examined
grounds, that there is such a being as the God
whom we adore—that he is the Creator and
Ruler of all things—that he has inspired prophets, evangelists, and apostles, to reveal his
justice and his grace to men—that the great
truth which constitutes the glory of his revelation, is the doctrine of the salvation of sinners
through faith in the Divine and incarnate
Redeemer's sacrifice—and that men are led to
rely on the sacrifice of Christ, to love, imitate,
and serve him, by the power of the Holy
Spirit working in them ;—we are perfectly
satisfied that these truths cannot be contradicted
by any other truths.   Beyond this, we are fully
convinced that every other truth bears some
relation to these truths, whether we can discover
their precise relation or not.   It follows that
there is no real science, no sound philosophy,
either in rejecting the gospel, or treating it with

indifference. It also follows, that there is no evangelical piety in disparaging science or in discouraging philosophy. One lesson, indeed, the Christian learns from Scripture, and it is confirmed both by his own experience, and by the experience of others, as brought under his personal observation, or learned by reading— namely, that there is spiritual danger in every employment of the intellect, when it becomes excessive, when it absorbs the whole attention, and when it is accompanied by disrelish for the humbling truths with which the gospel begins its teachings. There is danger, too, in being so fascinated with those studies which bring demonstration to the understanding, as to neglect those higher studies which make us feel the limitation of our intellectual powers, and the need of ONE to teach us, who clearly understands the unseen, spiritual, and eternal realities which lie beyond our range of experience or of specu- lation, and of which we can know nothing, but by lowly faith in the revelations of the infinite Mind.

If every study is pursued with a reference to that which is *itself* the highest, and *to us* the most pressing, and of most lasting interest, reason and revelation, science and faith, philo- osophy and piety, instead of seeming to be in-

consistent, will be felt to be harmonious. It is
well known that the ample fields of nature, in
the heavens and in the earth, can be intelligently
contemplated only by those whose minds are
trained to such employments, and that persons
not so trained are apt to regard all their wonderful statements—which they can prove to be
true — as scarcely worthy of belief, and as
of no practical use whatever in the daily
affairs of life. " The book of revelation,"
says sir David Brewster, "exhibits to us the
same peculiarities as that of nature. To the
ordinary eye it presents no immediate indications of its Divine origin. Events apparently insignificant—supernatural interferences,
seemingly unnecessary—doctrines almost con-
tradictory—and prophecies nearly ˙unintelligi-
ble, occupy its pages. The history of the fall of
man—of the introduction of moral and physical
evil—the prediction of a Messiah—the actual
advent of our Saviour—his instructions—his
miracles — his death — his resurrection — and
the subsequent propagation of his religion
by the unlettered fishermen of Galilee, are
each a stumbling-block to the wisdom of this
world. The youthful and vigorous mind,
when first summoned to peruse the Scriptures, turns from them with disappointment.

It recognises in them no profound science—no secular wisdom—no Divine eloquence—no disclosures of nature's secrets—no direct impress of an almighty Hand. But, though the system of revealed truth which this book contains is, like that of the universe, concealed from common observation, yet the labours of centuries have established its Divine origin, and developed, in all its order and beauty, the great plan of human restoration. In the chaos of its incidents we discover the whole history of our species, whether it is delineated in events that are past, or shadowed forth in those that are to come—from the creation of man, and the origin of evil, to the extinction of his earthly dynasty, and the commencement of his immortal career.

" The antiquity and authenticity of the books which contain the sacred canon — the fulfilment of its prophecies — the miraculous works of its Founder—his death and resurrection—have been demonstrated to all who are capable of appreciating the force of historical evidence ; and in the poetical and prose compositions of the inspired authors we discover a system of doctrine and a code of morality, traced in characters as distinct and legible as the most unerring truths in the material world. False systems of religion have, indeed, been

deduced from the sacred record, as false systems
of the universe have sprung from the study of
the book of nature ; but the very prevalence of
a false system proves the existence of one
which is true ; and though the two classes of
facts necessarily depend on different kinds of
evidence, yet we scruple not to say, that the
Copernican system is not more demonstrably
true than the system of theological truth contained in the Bible. If men of high powers,
then, are still found, who are insensible to the
evidence which sustains the system of the
universe, need we wonder that there are others,
whose minds are shut against the effulgent
evidence which entrenches the strongholds of
our faith ?

" If such, then, is the character of the Christian faith, we need not be surprised that it was
embraced and expounded by such a genius as
sir Isaac Newton. Cherishing its doctrines,
and leaning on its promises, he felt it his duty,
as it was his pleasure, to apply to it that intellectual strength which had successfully sur-
mounted the difficulties of the material universe.
The fame which that success procured him, he
could not but feel to be the breath of popular
applause, which administered only to his personal feelings ; but the investigation of the

sacred mysteries, while it prepared his own mind for its final destiny, was calculated to promote the spiritual interests of thousands. This noble impulse he did not hesitate to obey ; and, by thus uniting philosophy to religion, he dissolved the league which genius had formed with scepticism, and added to the cloud of witnesses the brightest name of ancient or of modern times."

It is but fair to other eminent writers of the same age as that which was adorned by Newton, to add that they, as well as he, combined the study of nature with the study of revelation. The names of Pascal, Boyle, Wallis, Hooke, Whiston, and Clarke, will readily occur ; and his great and German rival, Leibnitz, is as well known in the walks of theology as in the paths of science. Even the French astronomer, La Place, is reported to have expressed, not long before his death, to an eminent professor at Cambridge, his approbation of the union of religion and literature in the public education of England ; avowing his conclusion, that education, in order to be effective, must be connected with religion. He is said to have added : " You in England are not in subjection to Popery : *keep Popery down*." Other names may, perhaps, be remembered of men distinguished for their attainments in science, who, instead of consecrating their genius and their attainments to the service of God, have employed them in denying or deriding his " glorious gospel." It is a mournful truth ;—mournful that they, with all their bright intelligence, should have been strangers to the " things which are not seen," which " are eternal," which have not " entered into the heart of man," but which " God has revealed unto us by his Holy Spirit ; "—and mournful, too, because their brilliant names and their seductive examples are remembered as *excuses* for that neglect of the gospel, for which no valid *reason* has ever yet been offered. If they were wrong and unhappy in their dislike to truth, that does not turn the " truth into a lie." Some of them and of their followers have " repented at the last" of their unworthy treatment of the gospel ; but who has heard, at any time, that a well-informed, earnest, and consistent believer in Jesus Christ has abjured it. because he found it hollow, and unworthy of his confidence in the hour of trial, and in the approach of death ?

CHAPTER VIII.

The illness and supposed mental derangement of sir Isaac Newton.

A STORY appeared in Dodsley's Annual Register, in 1776, respecting the effect of an unexpected loss of some valuable papers on the mind of Newton. After the greater part of this story had been refuted and forgotten in England, it was revived in France, and accompanied with remarks which have been received by Englishmen and Christians with great displeasure, as reflecting on the wisdom of Newton, and disparaging the dignity of religion. The truth appears to be, that one morning, while he was at chapel, a favourite little dog, named Diamond, had accidentally set fire to some papers which had been left on his master's table. On discovering his loss, Newton is said to have cried out, " Oh ! Diamond, Diamond ! little do you know the mischief you have done me !" Among the papers destroyed was the manuscript of a book, containing the experiments which he had been making on light and colours for twenty years, and which he had nearly finished. The loss of his papers, together with other causes, painfully affected his health. In this state of depression, he wrote some letters to Mr. Pepys, secretary to the Admiralty, and to Mr. Locke, which show how seriously his nervous system had been deranged. His correspondents were perplexed. Mr. Millington, of Magdalene College, Cambridge, to whom Mr. Pepys had written to inquire about Newton's health, informed him that it was "a distemper that much seized his head, and kept him awake for above five nights together, which, upon occasion, he desired I would represent to you, and beg your pardon, he being very much ashamed he should be so rude to a person for whom he hath so great an honour. He is now very well, and though I fear he is under some small degree of melancholy, yet I think there is no reason to suspect that it hath at all touched his understanding, and I hope never will."

In Newton's correspondence with Locke, there is a letter written about the same time with that to Mr. Pepys, which contains Newton's own account of his state. " The last winter, by sleeping too often by my fire, I got an ill habit of sleeping; and a distemper, which this summer has been epidemical, put me further out of order, so that when I wrote to you I had not slept an hour a night for a fortnight together, and for five days not a wink. I remember I wrote to you, but what I said of your book I remember not. If you please to send me a transcript of that passage I will give you an account of it if I can." That so close a student should have suffered in his health, and that the effect of disease on his system should have been a serious disturbance of his calm tenor of feeling, can awaken no surprise. Nor is it unlikely that some severe trial of his patience was experienced about that time, by the delay of the existing government to honour him, as both himself and his friends had been led to expect. He had reached the summit of intellectual glory. It was during the period of his illness, however, that he composed his Letters to Dr. Bentley, which were mentioned in the last chapter. He was also occupied at the same time with some abstruse mathematical questions, as well as many delicate observations on haloes round the sun, which were afterwards published in his Treatise on Optics. During the same period, too, he was diligently employed in his duties at the Mint; while his

leisure hours were devoted to the improvement
of the " Principia," and to those other studies in
which philosophy yields to the supremacy of
faith, and hope administers to the aspirations
of genius.*

* Brewster's Life of Newton, p. 245.

CHAPTER IX.

ITALY was the birthplace of the societies and academies which contributed so largely, after the revival of learning in modern Europe, to the rapid spread of science. The Royal Society of London, instituted for the express purpose of advancing *experimental philosophy*, is acknowledged to be the most magnificent European establishment of this kind. It began with a few lovers of mathematics and natural philosophy, who met at first in London, then in Oxford, and finally at Gresham College, in London. The Royal Society was organized in 1660, and was constituted a body corporate by royal charter in 1662. Five years after, the Society received from Mr. Henry Howard, afterwards duke of Norfolk, the library which his grandfather, the earl of Arundel, had purchased at Vienna, together with convenient apartments for their meetings in Arundel

House, after Gresham College had been injured by the great fire. In about three years, they returned to Gresham College. For many years, they met in Crane-court, Fleet-street, but about the year 1792, the government devoted to their use the apartments in Somerset House in which their meetings still continue to be held. At the time when this Society was founded, England took the lead, especially in the mathematical sciences and in astronomy. Sir Isaac Newton was the twelfth president, and he held that office twenty-four years. The labours of the Society are embodied in the Transactions, which continued to be published in numbers until the appearance of the forty-sixth volume, in the year 1750. For twelve years after that time, a half volume was printed every year; but from 1762, the Society issued a complete volume every year. These papers are of varied importance; some among the earlier were trifling and worthless. They are ably condensed by Dr. Thomson, in his History of the Royal Society, and arranged under the following heads: 1. Natural History. 2. Mathematics. 3. Mechanical Philosophy. 4. Chemistry. 5. Miscellaneous Articles.

Some of the most important of Newton's discoveries were preceded and aided by those of

Dr. WALLIS, whose mathematical works, in three large volumes, were published during his life-time. Among these were the " Arithmetic of Infinites," which led the way to Mercator's ingenious discoveries, as well as Newton's, in the properties of curves. The Fluxions of Newton were more nearly approached by ISAAC BARROW, the nephew and the namesake of bishop Barrow.

After many changes, and much travelling in France, Italy, Turkey, Germany, and Holland, Newton returned to England after the restoration of Charles II. He expressed his disappointment at the king's neglect of him in two Latin lines, which may be thus expressed in English:—

> " No man had more longed for thy return,
> O Charles, and none has felt it less."

In about three years after Barrow came home, he was appointed Professor of Geometry in Gresham College, and in the following year was chosen, at the recommendation of Dr. Wilkins, the first mathematical professor in the chair founded at Cambridge, which he had occupied six years when he resigned it to Newton, devoting the remainder of his life to theology. Barrow became soon after the master of Trinity College, king Charles declaring that he had given the place to the best scholar in

England.   The university elected him vice-
chancellor in 1675, and in 1677 he died of
fever, being only forty-seven years old.   It is
said that he was a man of athletic size, yet of
mild disposition.   He is famous for his sermons.   The king used to call him his unfair
preacher, because when he discussed a subject
he so exhausted it, as to leave nothing for any
other preacher to do.   He was the author of
several Latin poems, but his fame rests mainly
on his mathematical writings.

Another fellow of the Royal Society in Newton's time was JAMES GREGORY, the inventor of
the reflecting telescope, and the author of a work
of great merit, on the " Quadrature of the Circle
and the Hyperbola," and of a " Treatise on Optics."

LEIBNITZ, though not a member of the
Royal Society, is so mixed with one of the
most important questions in Newton's connexion
with the Society, that a short account of him
seems to be required in this place.   Leibnitz
was a man of most comprehensive genius and
wonderfully varied attainments.   In 1673, he
was introduced to the leading fellows of the
Royal Society in London, and thus became
acquainted with some of the discoveries of
Newton.   He visited England at three separate
times.   His fondness for controversy, and his

disposition to arrogate to himself the inventions of others, will account for the attacks which he made on Newton, who, both as a man and as a philosopher, was greatly his superior. In the Philosophical Transactions for 1714, there is a remarkably calm comparison between them, which we believe to have come from Newton's own pen :—

"It must be allowed that these two gentlemen differ very much in philosophy. The one proceeds on the evidence arising from experiments and phenomena, and stops where such evidence is wanting; the other is taken up with hypotheses, and propounds them, not to be examined by experiments, but to be believed without examination. The one, for want of experiments to decide the question, does not affirm whether the cause of gravity be mechanical or not mechanical; the other, that it is a perpetual miracle, if it be not mechanical. The one, by way of inquiry, attributes it to the power of the Creator that the least particles of matter are hard; the other attributes the hardness of matter to conspiring motions, and calls it a perpetual miracle, if the cause of this hardness be other than mechanical. The one does not affirm that animal motion in man is purely mechanical; the other teaches that it is purely mechanical—

the soul or mind (according to the hypothesis of a *harmonia præstabilita*) never acting on the body so as to alter or influence its motions. The one teaches that God (the God in whom 'we live, and move, and have our being') is omnipresent, but not a soul of the world; the other, that he is *not the* soul of the world, but *intelligentia supramundana*—an intelligence above the bounds of the world; whence it seems to follow that he cannot do anything within the bounds of the world, unless by an incredible miracle. The one teaches, that philosophers are to argue from phenomena and experiments to the causes thereof, and thence to the causes of those causes, and so on till we come to the first cause; the other, that all the actions of the first cause are miracles, and all the laws impressed on nature by the will of God are perpetual miracles and occult qualities, and, therefore, not to be considered in philosophy. But, must the constant and universal laws of nature, if derived from the power of God, or the action of a cause yet unknown to us, be called miracles and occult qualities, that is to say, wonders and absurdities? Must all the arguments for a God, taken from the phenomena of nature, be exploded by new hard names? And must experimental philosophy be exploded as miraculous and absurd, because it asserts nothing more than can be proved by experiments, and we cannot yet prove by experiments that all the phenomena in nature can be solved by mere mechanical causes? Certainly these things deserve to be better considered."

The name of HUYGHENS, the prince of philosophers in Holland, has several times occurred in preceding chapters. Eminent as a mathematician, an astronomer, and a mechanician, he is chiefly celebrated for his discovery of the ring of Saturn, of one of the satellites of that planet, for his application of the pendulum to astronomical purposes, and his micrometer, which had also been invented in England by Gascoigne. It was Huyghens, too, who inferred, from some experiments with the pendulum, that the earth is an oblate spheroid, flattened at the poles—a theory which Newton had independently and previously demonstrated, from the doctrine of gravitation, on the assumption that the earth had been originally in a fluid state. This theory led to the well-known controversy between Newton and Cassini, which the French Academy of Sciences decided in Newton's favour, by measuring a degree of the earth's meridian in the torrid and in the frigid zone.

Dr. ROBERT HOOKE, the greatest mechanician
of his age, occupied a prominent place in the
Royal Society during the first thirty years of
its operations. He succeeded Mr. Oldenburg
as secretary, in 1677. He is said to have been
small and deformed in person, impracticable in
temper — arrogantly assuming the inventions
and discoveries of other men—a disappointed
man, and, in the later years of his life, bordering
on derangement. He invented the balance-
spring in watches about fourteen years before
it was made known by Huyghens.

FLAMSTEAD was the first astronomer royal in
the Observatory at Greenwich. He determined
the places of the fixed stars with more accuracy
than had been reached before his observations
were made.

Next to Newton himself, the most illustrious
member of the Royal Society was Dr. HALLEY.
Before he joined the Society, he had conceived
the design of drawing up a catalogue of the
stars in the southern hemisphere, and he spent
some time at the island of St. Helena for the
purpose of ascertaining their position. During
his abode in that island, he had an opportunity
of observing the transit of the planet Mercury
across the sun's disk. He went, after his
admission to the Royal Society, to join Hevilius

in making important telescopic observations at Danzig. It was while studying the planetary motions, and suspecting, as Dr. Hooke did, that gravitation was the probable cause of those motions, yet unable to detect the law according to which the power of gravity diminishes by distance, he consulted Dr. Hooke and sir Christopher Wren, but without satisfaction. He then took the memorable journey to Cambridge, which brought to light those theories on gravitation which he urged Newton to elaborate in his "Principia." Halley had become clerk to the Royal Society, and he drew up the greater part of its Philosophical Transactions. The year after the appearance of the "Principia," he explained the fact that the Mediterranean Sea does not increase, though so many great rivers flow into it, by the theory of evaporation. As the result of voyages to the African coast, the western shores of America, the West Indies, and other parts, he published his "General Chart," exhibiting at one view the variations of the compass in all the seas frequented by British navigators. He also published a large chart of the British Channel. He succeeded sir Hans Sloane as secretary to the Royal Society, and Flamstead as astronomer royal at Greenwich, in the sixty-fifth year of his age.

For more than twenty years, he devoted his active mind to the perfecting of the theory of the moon. It is related, that queen Caroline, the friend of Leibnitz and of Newton, frequently visited Halley at Greenwich. On one of these occasions, we are told, the queen expressed her regret that the salary of the office was so small, and offered to use her influence with the king to have it raised. Halley begged her majesty not to do so, " for," he said, " the consequence would be, that hereafter the situation may be granted to the younger son of some nobleman, unfit for the duty, but attracted merely by the emolument."

Mr. BOYLE's name is, perhaps, familiar to the reader. He was one of the original number of literary and scientific men who founded the Royal Society. His scientific tastes were directed to several departments of natural history, and more specially to chemistry, pneumatics, and hydrostatics. With the help of Dr. Hooke's mechanical ingenuity, he greatly improved the air-pump, which had been invented by Guericke.

ROGER COTES, whose correspondence with Newton respecting the " Principia" has been referred to, was a man of extraordinary abilities as a mathematician. He died at the age of thirty-four, greatly regretted by the scientific world.   Sir Isaac said of him, in reference to one of his beautiful inventions, "If he had lived, we might have known something." After his death, his papers were published by his cousin, Dr. Robert Smith, in a volume, entitled " *Harmonia Mensurarum*," the earliest work which displayed much progress in applying logarithms and the properties of the circle to the calculus of fluents.

This seems to be the proper place to introduce the Minutes of the Royal Society respecting sir Isaac Newton.

"1671, Dec. 23rd.—The lord bishop of Sarum proposed for candidate Mr. Isaac Newton, professor of mathematics at Cambridge.

"1672, January 11th.—Mr. Isaac Newton was elected.   At that meeting, mention was made of his improvement of telescopes by contracting them, and that *that* which himself had sent thither to be examined had been seen by the king, and considered also by the president, sir Robert Murray, sir Paul Neile, Dr. Christopher Wren, and Mr. Hooke, at Whitehall ; and that they had so good an opinion of it, as that they concluded a description and a scheme of it should be sent by the secretary, in a letter on purpose, to M. Huyghens at Paris, thereby to secure the contrivance to the author, who had also written a letter to Mr. Oldenburg from Cambridge, altering and enlarging the description of his instrument, which had been sent home for his review, before it should go abroad. This description was read, and ordered to be entered in the register-book, together with the scheme. The curator said he did endeavour to make such a telescope himself, and to find out a metal not obnoxious to tarnishing. It was ordered that a letter should be wrote by the secretary to Mr. Newton, to signify to him his election, and also to thank him for the communication of his telescope, and to assure him that the society would take care that all right should be done him in the matter of this invention.

" January 18th.—Mr. Newton's new telescope was examined and applauded.

" January 25th.—Mr. Oldenburg read a letter of Mr. Newton's, written to him from Cambridge, January 18th, concerning an intimation, first, of preparing a fit metalline matter for reflecting concaves; secondly, of a considerable philosophical discovery he intends to send to this society, to be considered and examined.

" February 2nd. — The third letter from Mr. Newton from Cambridge, about his discovery of the nature of light, refractions,

and colours; importing that light was not
a similar but heterogeneous thing, consist-
ing of difform rays, which had essentially
different refractions, abstracted from bodies
that they pass through; and that colours are
produced from such and such rays, whereof
some in their own nature are disposed to be
red, others blue, others purple, etc., and that
whiteness is nothing else but a mixture of all
sorts of colours blended together.

"Ordered, that the author be solemnly thanked,
in the name of the Society, for this very ingenious discourse, and be made acquainted that
the Society think very fit, if he consents, to
have it forthwith printed, as well for the greater
convenience of having it well considered by
philosophers, as for securing the considerable
notices thereof to the author against the arro-
gations of others. Ordered also, that the discourse be entered in the register-book, and
that the bishop of Salisbury, Mr. Boyle,
and Mr. Hooke, be desired to peruse and
consider it, and bring in a report of it to the
Society.

"March 28th.—There was read a letter of
Mr. Newton's, written to Mr. Oldenburg from
Cambridge, containing some more particulars
relating to his new telescope, especially the

proportions of the apertures, and changes for several lengths of that sort of telescope.

" April 4th.—The secretary read a letter of Mr. Newton's, written to him from Cambridge, concerning his answers to the difficulties objected by Mons. ———— about his reflecting telescope, as also to the queries of Mons. Denys concerning the same ; together with his proposal of a way of using, instead of a little oval metal, in that telescope, a crystal, figured like a triangular prism. Ordered, that the curator take care to make such a crystalline prism for the design mentioned, and to use the same.

" May 16th.—Mr. Hooke made some experiments relating to Mr. Newton's theory of light and colours, which he was desired to bring in writing to be registered.

" May 22nd.—Mr. Hooke made some more experiments with two prisms, confirming what Mr. Newton hath written in his discourse about light and colour, namely, that the rays of light being separated by one prism into distinct colours, the refraction made by another prism doth not alter these colours.

" 1675, November 18th.—Mr. Newton offering to send to the Society, in a letter dated November 13th, a discourse of his about colours, when it shall be thought convenient, the Society ordered the secretary to thank him for his offer, and to desire him to send the discourse as soon as he pleased.

" December 9th.—There was produced a manuscript of Mr. Newton's, touching his theory of light and colours, containing partly an hypothesis to explain the properties of light, by him discoursed of in his former papers, and partly the principal phenomena of the various colours exhibited by their plates or bubbles, esteemed by him to be of a more difficult consideration, yet to depend also on the said properties of light. Of the hypothesis there was read only the first part, giving an account of refraction, reflexion, transparency, and opacity ; the second part, explaining colours, was referred to the next meeting.

" December 16th.—The sequel of his hypothesis, which was begun to be read the last day, was read to the end. To which Mr. Hooke said, that the main of it was contained in his 'Micrography,' which Mr. Newton, in some particulars, had only carried further.

" 1676, January 10th.—Read a letter of Mr. Newton's, written to Mr. Oldenburg, December 20th, 1675, stating the difference between his hypothesis and that of Mr. Hooke, in his 'Micrography,' the result of which is, that he (Mr. Newton) hath nothing in common with Mr. Hooke, but a supposition that ether is a medium susceptible of vibrations, of which supposition Mr. Newton saith he makes quite a different use—Mr. Hooke supposing it light itself, which Mr. Newton does not. Besides that, he explains very differently from Mr. Hooke the manner of refraction and reflection, and the nature and productions of colours in all cases, and even in the colours of transparent substances. Mr. Newton says he explains everything in a way so differing from Mr. Hooke, that the experiments he grounds his discourse upon destroy all Mr. Hooke saith about them. And that the two main experiments, without which the manner of the production of these colours is not to be found out, were not only unknown to Mr. Hooke, when he wrote his ' Micrography,' but even last spring, as he understood by mentioning them to the said Mr. Hooke. Read the beginning of Mr. Newton's discourse, containing such observations as conduce to further discoveries, for completing his theory of light and colours, especially as to the constitution of natural bodies on which their colour and transparency depend, in which discourse he first describes the principal of his observations, and then considers and makes use of them.

" January 20th.—At this time were read the first fifteen observations, which did so well please the company that they ordered the secretary to desire the author would permit them to be published, together with the rest, which they presumed did correspond to those that had now been read to them.

" January 27th.—Mr. Newton's letter of January 5th was read, wherein he acknowledges the favour of the Society in the kind acceptance of his late papers, and declares that he knows not how to deny anything which they desire should be done; only he desires that the printing (of) his observations upon colours may be suspended awhile, because he has some thoughts of writing another set of observations for determining the manner of production of colours by the prism, which observations, he says, ought to precede those now in our hands, and will do best joined with them.

"February 3rd.—The reading of Mr. Newton's discourse was continued, namely, that part wherein he explains the simplest of colours by the more compounded.

" February 10th.—There was read the last part of Mr. Newton's discourse, wherein is considered, in nine propositions, how the phenomena of thin transparent plates stand related to those of a natural bodies, in which he inquires after their constitutions, whereby they reflect some rays more copiously than others.

"1684, December 10th.—Mr. Halley gave an account that he had lately seen Mr. Newton at Cambridge, and that he had shown him a curious treatise, '*De Motu Corporum*,' ['On the Motion of Bodies',] which, upon his desire, he said was promised to be sent to the Society to be entered upon their register. Mr. Halley was desired to put Mr. Newton in mind of his promise, for securing his invention to himself, till such time as he can be at leisure to publish it. Mr. Paget was desired to join with Mr. Halley.

"February 25th.—A letter was read from Mr. Newton, concerning his willingness to promote a philosophical meeting at Cambridge, the entering in our register his notions about motion, and his intentions to fit them suddenly for the press.

"1686, April 28th.—*Dr. Vincent presented the Society with a* MS. *treatise, entitled* 'PHILOSOPHIÆ NATURALIS PRINCIPIA MATHEMATICA,' *and dedicated to the Society by* MR. IS. NEWTON; *wherein he gives a mathematical demonstration of the Copernican hypothesis, as proposed by Kepler, and makes out all the phenomena of the celestial motions, by the only supposition of a gravitation towards the centre of the sun, decreasing as the squares of the distances therefrom reciprocally.*

" May 19th.—Ordered that Mr. Newton's book be printed forthwith, in a quarto of a fair letter; and that a letter be written to him to signify the Society's resolution, and to desire his opinion as to the print, volume, cuts, etc.

" June 2nd.—Ordered that Mr. Newton's book be printed, and that Mr. Edm. Halley shall undertake the business of looking after it, and printing it *at his own charge, which he engaged to do.*

" January 26th.—Ordered that Mr. Newton be consulted whether he designs to treat of the opposition of the medium to bodies moving in it, in his treatise '*De Motu Corporum*,' now in the press.

" 1692. February 1st.—There was produced Mr. Newton's and Dr. Gregory's quadrature of curved lines, both of which will be printed in Dr. Wallis's Latin edition of his 'Algebra.' It was chiefly a proposition sent to Dr. Gregory from Mr. Newton, much about the time, Dr. Gregory says, he discovered it himself, being a method of squaring all curved lines that are expressible in any binomial. Mr. Newton has subjoined a like rule, when it cannot be expressed under a trinomial, and mentioned that his process will go on *ad infinitum*, and square the curve when the ordinate cannot be expressed without an infinite series.

" 1694, July 4th.—Ordered, that a letter be written to Mr. Newton, praying that he will please to communicate to the Society, in order to be printed, his Treatise of Light and Colours, and what other mathematical or physical treatises he has ready by him.

" October 31st.—Dr. Halley said that Mr. Newton had lately told him, that there was reason to conclude that the bulk of the earth did grow and increase in magnitude by the perpetual accession of new particles, attracted out of the ether by its gravitating power, and he supposed, and proposed to the Society, that this increase of the *moles* of the earth would occasion an acceleration of the moon's motion, she being at this time attracted by a stronger *vis centripeta* than in remote ages.

" A letter from M. Leibnitz to Mr. Bridges was read, wherein he recommends to the Society to use their endeavours to induce Mr. Newton to publish his further thoughts and improvements on the subject of his late book, ' *Principia Philosophiæ Mathematicæ*,' and his other physical and mathematical discoveries ; lest, by his death, they should happen to be lost.

" 1703, November 4th.—Sir Isaac Newton

chosen of the Council, and PRESIDENT, the same day.

"February 16th.— The president presented his book of 'Optics' to the Society. Mr. Halley was desired to peruse it, and to give an abstract of it ; and the Society gave the president thanks for the book, and for being pleased to publish it.

" 1711. — Mr. Keill observed, that in the Leipzig ' *Acta Eruditorum*' for the year 1705, there is an unfair account given of sir Isaac Newton's 'Discourse of Quadratures,' asserting the method of demonstration there by him made use of to M. Leibnitz, etc. Upon which the president gave a short account of that matter, with the particular time of his first mentioning or discovering his invention, referring to some letters published by Dr. Wallis ; upon which Mr. Keill was desired to draw up an account of the matters in dispute, and set it in a just light.

"May 24th.—A letter from Mr. John Keill to Dr. Sloane was produced and read, relating to the dispute concerning the priority of invention of the arithmetic of fluxions, between sir Isaac Newton and M. Leibnitz, wherein Mr. Keill asserts the president's claim, etc. A copy of this letter was ordered to be sent to M. Leibnitz,

and Dr. Sloane was desired to draw up a letter
to accompany it, before it was made public in
the Transactions, which should not be till after
the receipt of M. Leibnitz's answer.

"1711, January 31st.—A letter from M. Leibnitz to Dr. Sloane was read, in which he com-
plains of Mr. Keill's unfair dealing with him in
his last letter, relating to the dispute between
him and sir Isaac Newton : the letter was delivered to the president to consider the contents
thereof.

" March 11th. — Upon account of M.
Leibnitz's letter to Dr. Sloane, concerning the
disputes formerly mentioned, a committee was
appointed by the Society to inspect the letters
and papers relating thereto, namely, Dr. Ar-
buthnot, Mr. Hill, Dr. Halley, Mr. Jones, Mr.
Machin, and Mr. Burnet, who were to make
their report to the Society.

"1712, April 24th. — The committee appointed to inspect the papers, letters, and books
of the Society, on account of the dispute
between M. Leibnitz and Mr. Keill, delivered
in their report, which was read, as follows :—

" We have consulted the letters and letter-
books in the custody of the Royal Society, and
those found amongst the papers of Mr. John
Collins, dated between the years 1669 and

1677, inclusive, and showed them to such as knew and avowed the hands of Mr. Barrow, Mr. Collins, M. Oldenburg, and M. Leibnitz, and compared those of Mr. Gregory with one another, and with copies of some of them, taken in the hand of Mr. Collins, and have extracted from them what relates to the matter referred to us ; all which extracts herewith delivered to you, we believe to be genuine and authentic ; and, by these letters and papers, we find :—

" 1st. That M. Leibnitz was in London in the beginning of the year 1673, and went hence, in or about March, to Paris, where he kept a correspondence with Mr. Collins, by means of M. Oldenburg, till about September, 1676, and then returned by London and Amsterdam to Hanover ; and that Mr. Collins was very free in communicating to able mathematicians what he had received from Mr. Newton and Mr. Gregory.

" 2nd. That when M. Leibnitz was the first time in London, he contended for the invention of another differential method, properly so called ; and, notwithstanding that he was shown by Mr. Pell that it was Newton's method, he persisted in maintaining it to be his own invention, by reason that he had found it by himself, without knowing what Newton had done before, and had much improved it ; and we find no mention of his having any other differential method than Newton's before his letter of June 21st, 1677, which was a year after a copy of Mr. Newton's letter, of December 10th, 1672, had been sent to Paris to be communicated to him ; and above four years after Mr. Collins began to communicate that letter to his correspondents, in which letter the method of fluxions was sufficiently described to any intelligent person.

" 3rd. That, by Mr. Newton's letter of June 13th, 1676, it appears that he had the method of fluxions above five years before the writing of that letter ; and, by his ' *Analysis per Equationes Numero Terminorum Infinitas*,' communicated by Dr. Barrow to Mr. Collins in July, 1669, we find that he had invented the method before that time.

" 4th. That the *differential* method is one and the same with the method of fluxions, excepting the name and mode of notation ; M. Leibnitz calling these quantities *differences* which Mr. Newton calls *moments* or *fluxions*, and marking them with the letter d, a mark not used by Mr. Newton. We therefore take the proper question to be—not who invented this or that method, but who was the FIRST *inventor of the* method ; and we believe that those who had reputed M. Leibnitz the first inventor know little or nothing of his correspondence with Mr. Collins and M. Oldenburg long before, nor of Mr. Newton's having the method above fifteen years before M. Leibnitz began to publish it in the ' *Acta Eruditorum* ' of Leipzig.

" For which reason we reckon Mr. Newton the FIRST *inventor*, and are of opinion that Mr. Keill, in asserting the same, has been no way injurious to M. Leibnitz ; and we submit it to the judgment of the Society, whether the extract of the letters and papers now presented, together with what is extant to the same purpose in Dr. Wallis's third volume, may not deserve to be made public.

" To which report the Society agreed *nem. con.*, and ordered that the whole matter, from the beginning, with the extracts of all the letters relating thereto, and Mr. Keill's and M. Leibnitz's letters, be published with all convenient speed that may be, together with the report of the said committee.

" Ordered, that Dr. Halley, Mr. Jones, and Mr. Machin, be desired to take care of the said impression, (which they promised,) and Mr. Jones to make an estimate of the charges, against the next meeting.

"1713, January 8th.—Some copies of the book entitled ' *Commercium Epistolicum*,' etc., printed by the Society's order, being brought, the president ordered one to be delivered to each person of the committee for that purpose, to examine it before its publication."

It may interest the reader to have a list of the presidents of the Royal Society from its foundation, in 1663, to the present time:—

1663. William lord Brouncker.
1677. Sir Joseph Williamson, knt.
1680. Sir Christopher Wren, knt.
1682. Sir John Hoskins, bart.
1683. Sir Cyril Wyche, bart.
1684. Samuel Pepys, esq.
1686. John, earl of Cosbery.
1689. Thomas, earl of Pembroke and Montgomery.
1690. Sir Robert Southwell, knt.
1695. Charles Montague, esq. (afterwards earl of Halifax.)
1698. John, lord Somers.
1703. Sir Isaac Newton, knt.
1727. Sir Hans Sloane, bart.
1744. Martin Folkes, esq.
1752. George, earl of Macclesfield.
1764. James, earl of Morton.
1768. James Barrow, esq.
—— James West, esq.
1772. James Barrow, esq.
—— Sir Joseph Pringle, bart.
1778. Sir Joseph Bankes.
1820. Sir Humphrey Davy, bart.
1827. Davies Gilbert, esq.
1830. H. R. H. the duke of Sussex.
1838. The marquis of Northampton.
1851. The earl of Rosse.

A history of the Royal Society was published in 1667 by Dr. Sprat, afterwards bishop of Rochester. About a hundred years after, a larger history was published by Dr. Thomas Bird. In 1800, Dr. Thomson's history was published in one volume, 4to.*

For many years, nearly all the science of Great Britain may be said to have centred in the Royal Society; but, in the course of years, numerous associations, pursuing in detail most of the same objects, have been established in London, Edinburgh, Dublin, in the principal towns of the three kingdoms, and in the United States of America. Of all these associations the Royal Society of London may be justly regarded as the parent, and by them all it continues to be regarded with respect and veneration.

* The latest History is in the volumes, by C. R. Wied, esq., assistant secretary and librarian to the Society, published in 1848.

CHAPTER X.

No desire is more natural, or more common, than that of being acquainted with the external aspect, the figure, complexion, and features of men by whose genius, learning, or labours in any important sphere, the world has been improved and benefited. Mr. Conduit, who married Newton's niece, and who lived in sir Isaac's house during the latter part of his life, describes him thus : " He had a very lively and piercing eye, a comely and gracious aspect, with a fine head of hair, as white as silver, without any baldness, and, when his peruke was off, was a venerable sight." Bishop Atterbury, speaking of the later period of his life, represents him as having a languid look and manner. This opinion of bishop Atterbury is confirmed by an observation of Mr. Thomas Hearne, who says " that sir Isaac was a man of no very promising aspect. He was a short

well-set man. He was full of thought, and
spoke very little in company, so that his conversation was not agreeable. When he rode
in his coach, one arm would be out of his
coach one side, and the other on the other."
Sir Isaac never wore spectacles, and never
" lost more than one tooth to the day of his
death."*

His portrait, painted by sir Godfrey Kneller,
would seem to justify Mr. Conduit's description, though there is little expression in the
features beyond a calm and stedfast look. In
the Pepysian Collection at Cambridge there is
a remarkable drawing of Newton, in Indian ink,
which represents him without his " peruke,"
and suggests the idea of a thin person with
large and strong features, and suffering either
from pain, or intense thought, or both. This
interesting drawing is engraved by Outrim, and
is prefixed to Mr. Edleston's publication of
Newton's Correspondence with Cotes and other
eminent men. Mr. Edleston says respecting
it, " . . . This portrait may be considered as the
most interesting of all the known portraits of
our philosopher, as representing him at a time
of life the least remote from those memorable
eighteen months which it cost him to produce

* Sir David Brewster's Life of Newton, p. 342.

the great work that has immortalized his name."

It was Newton's habit, at Cambridge, to spend nearly his whole time in his chamber, relieving his severer studies by turning to history, chronology, chemistry, and theology. During his residence in London, he was exemplary in his attention to business, and to the courtesies of social life. He was seldom alone without a book before him, and a pen in his hand. His manner of living was not ostentatious, yet it was of the same style with that of other gentlemen of rank and fortune. Simple in his dress, and frugal in his meals, his hospitality was generous, and at times magnificent. As he never married, his management of his income enabled him to acquire considerable wealth. Instead of hoarding, he generously supplied, during his life, the wants of his relatives. To one he gave £800 ; to another, £200 ; to a third, £100 ; besides often assisting them with smaller sums, and entering into pecuniary engagements for their benefit. His donations to churches and chapels at Cambridge, and elsewhere, were numerous and liberal ; and he was habitually generous to the poor. It is mentioned in the Life of Colin Maclaurin, a fellow of the Royal Society, and

professor of mathematics in the university of
Edinburgh, who published an account of sir
Isaac Newton's Philosophical Discoveries—that
Newton interested himself greatly in securing
him the appointment to that chair. In one of
his letters to him he says: " I am very glad to
hear that you have a prospect of being joined
to Mr. James Gregory in the professorship of
the mathematics at Edinburgh, not only because
you are my friend, but principally because of
your abilities, you being acquainted as well
with the new improvements of mathematics as
with the former state of those sciences. I
heartily wish you good success, and shall be
very glad to hear of your being elected. I am,
with all sincerity, your faithful friend and most
humble servant."

Without informing Maclaurin, Newton wrote
also to the lord provost of Edinburgh : " I am
glad to understand that Mr. Maclaurin is in
good repute amongst you for his skill in mathematics, for I think he deserves it very well ;
and to satisfy you that I do not flatter him, and
also to encourage him to accept the place of
assisting Mr. Gregory, in order to succeed him,
I am ready (if you please to give me leave) to
contribute twenty pounds *per annum* towards a
provision for him, till Mr. Gregory's place

become void, if I live so long ; and I will pay
it to his order in London."

Sir Isaac Newton's personal estate was calculated at £32,000, which he divided among the
grandchildren of his mother and the reverend
Mr. Smith.   In his intercourse with society he
is described by those who knew him best as
remarkably free from all those eccentricities,
which so frequently disfigure the conduct of
men of genius.   Without exciting even a sus-
picion of vanity or malice, he adapted himself to
the condition and capacity of those with whom
he conversed.   Both his superior intelligence
and his considerate benevolence were transparent.   His estimate of himself was seen to be
modest.   He received the opinions of others,
and judged of their actions, with dignified candour.   A beautiful illustration of these features
in his character is given by Dr. Pemberton,
who succeeded Mr. Cotes in superintending the
publication of his "Principia" when a new edition
was required, and to whom the world is indebted for his popular " Account of Sir Isaac
Newton's Discoveries."   " But this," he says,
" I immediately discovered in him, which at
once surprised and charmed me.   Neither his
extreme great age, nor his universal reputation,
had rendered him stiff in opinion, or in any

degree elated.   Of this I had occasion to have
almost daily experience.   The remarks I continually sent him by letters on the " Principia,"
were received with the utmost goodness.   These
were so far from being any ways displeasing to
him, that, on the contrary, it occasioned him to
speak many kind things of me to my friends,
and to honour me with a public testimony of
his good opinion."   In perfect accordance with
this representation is the memorable language
of the great philosopher, on speaking of himself.   During the last ten years of his life,
when consulted about any passage in his works,
his reply was, "Address yourself to M. de
Moivie ; he knows that better than I do."   And
then, when his surrounding friends testified to
him the just admiration his discoveries had
universally excited, he said: " I know not
what the world may think of my labours ; but,
to myself, it seems that I have been but as a
child playing on the sea-shore ; now finding
some pebble rather more polished, and now
some shell rather more agreeably variegated
than another, while the *immense ocean of truth
extended itself* unexplored before me."

Newton was sincerely attached to the Church
of England ; but he cherished no bitterness
towards Nonconformists.   He judged of men

by their actions. Far from being satisfied with the sublime truths of natural theology, which he had studied more profoundly and more closely than all other men, he was an enlightened and humble believer in revelation ; and among the books of every kind with which he was familiar, the one which he read with the greatest assiduity was—the Bible. It is stated by a French writer, that, at a time of great political perplexity, king William was advised to take Newton into his council, and that the king replied, " Newton is nothing but a philosopher." The same writer wittily remarks, that in other circumstances Newton might have said of his majesty, " He is nothing but a politician ! " Dr. Maskelyne told professor Rigaud of Oxford, that when Dr. Halley ventured to say anything disrespectful to religion, Newton invariably checked him and said, " I have studied these things—you have not."

Though we have described Newton as remarkably free from eccentricities, it is not surprising that a man constantly engaged in the most abstruse and complicated studies, should sometimes need to be reminded that his meals were prepared. It is said that his friend Dr. Stukely called upon him one day, when his

dinner was already served up.   Having waited
some time, and becoming impatient, the doctor
removed the cover from a chicken, which he
presently ate, returning the bones to the dish,
and replacing the cover.   After a short time,
Newton came into the dining-room, and, after
usual compliments, sat down to dinner ; but
seeing only the bones of the bird, he observed,
with an expression of surprise, "I thought I had
not dined !"   The simplicity of his character
shows itself in the most amiable light, in a letter
which he wrote to Locke during the illness
mentioned in a former chapter :—

"Sir,—Being of opinion that you endeavoured
to embroil me with women, and by other means
I was so much affected with it, as that, when
one told me you were sickly, and would not live,
I answered, 'twere better if you were dead.   I
desire you to forgive me this uncharitableness,
for I am now satisfied that what you have done
is just, and I beg your pardon for my having
hard thoughts of you for it, and for representing that you struck at the root of morality, in
a principle you laid in your book 'of Ideas,' and
designed to pursue in another book ; and that
I took you for a Hobbist.   I beg your pardon,
also, for saying or thinking that there was a
design to sell me an office, or to embroil me.

I am, your most humble and unfortunate servant, ISAAC NEWTON."

Though Newton had suffered occasionally from gout, and, at one time, was greatly deranged in general health, his constitution was maintained in tolerable comfort till he had reached the age of fourscore. Then he suffered from stone. Even at that advanced age, however, he had intervals of good health and bodily comfort, and he improved greatly by removing his residence to Kensington. At that period, he had a remarkable conversation with his niece's husband, Mr. Conduit, which sir David Brewster has printed, from Turnor's " Collections," in the appendix to Newton's life : " He was better after it, (a fit of gout,) and had his head clearer and memory stronger than I had known them for some time. He then repeated to me, by way of discourse, very distinctly, though rather in answer to my queries than in one continued narration, what he had often hinted to me before. I asked him why he would not publish his conjectures *as* conjectures, and instanced that Kepler had communicated his ; and, though he had not gone so far as Kepler, yet Kepler's guesses were so just and happy, that they had been proved and demonstrated by *him.* His answer was, *I do not deal in conjectures.*"

About this time, he wished to resign his office in the Mint to Mr. Conduit, an arrangement which was effected after his death. On the 28th of February, 1727, he came to London for the last time, that he might preside at a meeting of the Royal Society. So well did he seem, that he had slept, only two nights before, from eleven till eight in the morning ; but he was so overcome with the fatigue of attending the meeting, and of receiving and paying visits, that, on returning to Kensington on the following Saturday, he was again seized with a violent attack of his distressing complaint. These paroxysms of agony forced drops of sweat down his face ; he bore them with the most placid fortitude, and resumed his usual cheerfulness when they passed away. For some days he appeared to rally, and on his last day but one, he displayed his ordinary vigour of mind in a long conversation with Dr. Mead. As the day declined, however, he fell into a state of insensibility, which continued for about twenty hours, when he died. He had lived more than eighty-five years. On the eleventh day after his decease, the body of sir Isaac Newton lay in state in the Jerusalem Chamber, and it was thence removed to Westminster Abbey. The grave is on the left hand, near the entrance to the choir.   At the funeral, sir Michael Newton, knight of the Bath, was chief mourner ; he was followed by other relatives, and some of the most distinguished personal friends of the departed.   The pall-bearers, fellows of the Royal Society, were the lord high chancellor, the duke of Roxburghe, the duke of Montrose, the earl of Pembroke, the earl of Sussex, and the earl of Macclesfield.   The bishop of Rochester performed the service, assisted by a prebend and the choir of the abbey.   In the most conspicuous part of that great temple stands his monument, erected in 1731, at the cost of £500, by his relations.   The following is an exact translation of the Latin inscription :—

Here lies
Sir Isaac Newton, knight,
who, by a vigour of mind almost supernatural,
first demonstrated
the motions and figures of the planets,
the paths of comets, and the tides of the ocean.
He diligently investigated
the different refrangibilities of the rays of light,
and the properties of colours to which they give rise.
An assiduous, sagacious, and faithful interpreter
of nature, antiquity, and the Holy Scriptures,
he asserted in his philosophy the majesty of God,
and exhibited in his conduct the simplicity of the gospel.
Let mortals congratulate themselves
That there has existed such, and so great
AN ORNAMENT OF THE HUMAN RACE.
Born, 25th Dec., 1642; died, 20th March, 1727.

The beautiful statue by Roubilliac, which

adorns the entrance to Trinity College chapel
at Cambridge, was the gift of Dr. Robert Smith,
professor of astronomy in that university. The
pedestal on which the statue is placed expresses
in one line the eulogy of Newton :—

> " Qui genus humanum ingenio superavit."
> [" Who excelled the human race in genius."]

> " Behold, a prism within his hands,
>   Absorbed in thought, great Newton stands ;
>   Such was his brow, and look serene,
>   His serious gait, and musing mien,
>   When taught on eagles' wings to fly,
>   He traced the wonders of the sky,
>   The chambers of the sun explored,
>   Where tints of thousand hues are stored."

" The family estates of Woolsthorpe and
Sustem, he bequeathed to John Newton, the
heir-at-law, whose grandfather was sir Isaac's
uncle. This gentleman does not seem to have
sufficiently valued the bequest, for he sold
them, in 1732, to Edmund Turnor of Stoke
Rochford. A short time before his death, sir
Isaac gave away an estate in Berkshire, to the
sons and daughter of Mrs. Conduit, who, in
consequence of their father dying before sir
Isaac, had no share in the personal estate ; and
he also gave an estate of the same value, which
he bought at Kensington, to Catherine, the only
daughter of Mr. Conduit, who afterwards married

Mr. Wallop, the eldest son of lord Lymington.
This lady was afterwards viscountess Lymington, and the estate of Kensington descended to
the late earl of Portsmouth, by whom it was
sold."*

* Sir David Brewster's Life of Newton, pp. 326, 327.

CHAPTER XI.

The intellectual superiority of Newton—His rigid method of inquiry—The magnificence of the results—The true position of Newton among philosophers—Testimonies to his fame.

THE praises which would be deemed extravagant when applied to any other man, are acknowledged by the most competent judges, in other nations as well as in our own, to be no more than simple truth when pronounced upon the genius of Newton. While other men have attained a glorious reputation by their military prowess, their daring adventures, their poetical creations, their learning, their ingenious conjectures, or the sagacity of their counsels in the great arena of public affairs, Newton's superiority is of a kind altogether different, and he stands alone in the brilliant and ever-widening circle of human greatness.

The most remarkable and characteristic features of his intellect are—his power of glancing at once into the very pith and marrow of the difficult questions that engaged his attention; his singular cautiousness in rejecting every plausible speculation; his unequalled power of continued and sustained thought on the most abstruse and complex investigations; his facility of rapid generalization, reducing an apparently confused heap of facts to harmony; and his penetration into the great principle or law by which this harmony is secured and maintained. Each of these properties was itself enough to have raised him, in that respect, above his fellow mortals; but that which made him what he really was, and what no other man whom we know of has been, was the combination and due proportion of them all. He did not reason, from some assumed principle, that the universe *must* be in accordance with his logical conclusions; nor did he conjecture, from some bright fancy which allured him, that it *might* be as he supposed; but he looked at the earth and at the heavens, gathered into a focus all the light which had been thrown upon them by previous inquirers, tested the accuracy of their observations and the safety of their methods, and then, calmly observing for himself the silent and steady revolutions of the heavenly bodies, patiently analysing the nature of light, the laws of motion, the properties of the curves in which the heavenly bodies move, the action of bodies and of the particles of which they consist, he arrived at the proportions of distances to times ; and by demonstrating the *law* of such proportions according to mathematical reasoning, confirmed by patient observation of *things as they are*, he solved the great mystery of the physical universe.

It is most true that the path had been opened to him by the illustrious mathematicians and astronomers who preceded him. It were idle to conjecture what such a mind as Newton's would have done if the way had not been thus prepared. The fact is, that all which had been done was nothing more than preparation for the great discoveries with which his name is inseparably associated. We cannot help observing, that there was one quality of mind which Newton possessed in a singular degree, to which he seems to have been indebted, probably even more than to those which have been particularized, for his pre-eminent success—his *humility*. On this point we quote the language of one who knew him well, and who drank deeply of his philosophy. " He avoided presumption. He had the necessary patience, as well as genius ; and having kept steadily to the right path, he therefore succeeded. . . . .

He has taken care to give nothing for demonstration but what must ever be found just; and having separated from this what he knows is not so certain, he has opened matter for the inquiries of future ages, which may confirm and enlarge his doctrines, but can never refute them.   He knew where to stop when experiments were wanting, and when the subtilty of nature carried things out of his reach; nor would he abuse the great authority and reputation he had acquired by delivering his opinion or conjectures otherwise than as matter of *question.*   It was long before he could be prevailed on to propose his opinion or conjectures concerning gravity; and what he has said of it, and of the other powers that act on the minute particles of matter, is delivered with a modesty and diffidence seldom to be met with amongst philosophers of a less name. . . . . The variety of opinions and perpetual disputes amongst philosophers has induced not a few, of late as well as in former times, to think that it was vain labour to endeavour to acquire certainty in natural knowledge, and to ascribe this to some unavoidable defect in the principles of the science.   But it has appeared sufficiently, from the disclosures of those who have consulted *nature,* and *not their own imaginations,* and particularly from what we learn from sir Isaac Newton, that the fault has lain in the *philosophers themselves*, and not in philosophy. A complete system, indeed, was not to be expected from one man or one age, or perhaps from the greatest number of ages; could we have expected it from the abilities of any one man, we surely should have had it from sir Isaac Newton; *but he saw too far into nature to attempt it.*"*

We can scarcely dwell too strongly on this peculiarity of Newton. It is not presumptuous, perhaps, to say that the great Author of nature cannot be approached without humility in the knowledge of his works, as we are well assured, from his own revelation, he will not be approached in that higher knowledge in which "standeth our eternal life." He seems to have ordained that there shall be a harmony between the intellectual faculties by which truth is learned, and the *disposition* with which those faculties are used. Humility is, itself, the moral confession of a truth, and of that truth which is most nearly concerned with our relation to God, and with our devout and reverential feeling towards him. Happy is it for the world,

* Account of sir Isaac Newton's Discoveries. By C. Maclaurin. 1775.

for philosophy, for religion, for all that elevates and blesses humanity, that the most highly gifted of philosophers was the humblest. Thinking of the magnitude of the universe, stretching his ample powers to their utmost verge, to catch the truth which everything exemplified, and waiting for its illuminations, he found, as lord Bacon quaintly expresses it, " that philosophy, like Jacob's vision, discovers to us a ladder, whose top reaches up to the footstool of the throne of God."

It is a proof of Newton's humility of mind, that he pursued with so much patience the culture of his own intellect by indefatigable study, and that he laboured so assiduously in those lower departments of ingenuity which have but slight attractions to speculative and brilliant men, but which, as employed by him, become dignified and noble. The grinding of glasses, the testing of metals, the construction of telescopes and microscopes, the persevering use of prisms and innumerable other instruments, were occupations which, however trifling they may seem to the superficial, were the very acts which proved the transcendent and overmastering love of truth, and which slowly, yet surely, led to its attainment. " He knew how to transfer the truths of abstract science to the study of things actually existing, and, by returning in the opposite direction, to enrich the former by ideas from the latter.

" In experimental and inductive investigation he was as great as in pure mathematics, and his discoveries were as distinguished in the one as in the other. In this double claim to renown, Newton stands unrivalled ; and though in the pure mathematics perhaps equals may be found, no one will come forwards as his rival both in that science and in the philosophy of nature." *
It is difficult to express in language sufficiently popular and brief for this publication, the extent and variety of the discoveries made by sir Isaac Newton. He invented the *reflecting telescope*, of which the idea had been partially realized by Gregory, and the quadrant. He discovered the properties and the analysis of *light*, and the nature of *colours*. He was the first to demonstrate that the rainbow is a natural prism, of which Playfair says, " There is not, perhaps, in the whole range of science, any instance of happier application of theory, or one in which the mind rests with fuller confidence." He was the *first* inventor of fluxions— the law by which the quadrature of all curves may be solved, also of incalculable value in the

* Playfair's "Second Dissertation," p. 89.

calculations upon the accuracy of which so much depends in the science of astronomy. He raised the doctrine of gravity from a vague conjecture to a rigid demonstration of the precise measure of the centripetal and centrifugal forces; ascertained the law according to which these forces act; proved that this law pervades alike the smallest particles and the largest masses; and, by means of this law, described the actual movements and orbits of the heavenly bodies, and explained the true configuration of the earth, the inequalities of planetary motions, the action of disturbing forces, the theory of the tides, the precession of the equinoxes, and the magnitude and density of the planets. " Thus it is found that the laws of motion and the general properties of matter are the same in the heavens and in the earth; that the elliptical motions of the primary and secondary planets—the small deviations from these motions, whether in the places of the planets or in the form and position of their orbits—the facts which concern their figures, their rotation, and the position of their axis; and, lastly, the oscillation of the waters which surround the earth, are all explained by ONE PRINCIPLE—' that of the mutual gravitation of all bodies, with forces *directly* as their quantities of matter, and *inversely* as the squares of their distances.' The existence of this force was not *assumed* as a hypothesis, but deduced as a necessary consequence from the general facts or laws discovered by Kepler. We have thus arrived at the knowledge of a principle which pervades all nature, and connects together the most distant regions of space, as well as the most remote periods of duration."*   In his pursuit of the great law of attraction, he examines the interior structure of bodies not less critically than their external motions, and he thus opened that bright way in the career of discovery in which chemistry has explained the combination of the particles of which all fluids and all solids are composed, by proving that chemical affinities and elective attractions are to be resolved into the same great principle which explains the greater movements of the physical universe.

Now, whatever comprehensiveness, and sagacity, and perseverance of intellect, Newton displayed in making these vast discoveries, it is worthy of observation, that there was nothing in the materials on which he had to work, or in the *method* on which he worked, that had not been known to Copernicus, to Tycho Brahe, to Galileo, and even to the impatient, imaginative, and presumptuous pretenders to philosophy

* Playfair's "Outlines of Natural Philosophy," vol. ii. p. 339.

in later times; but he excelled all other philosophers, whether real or pretended, in the *humility
of mind* which has been pointed out.   " Had he
been like the majority of other men, he would
have broken free from the fetters of a sober and
chastised understanding, and, giving wing to
his imagination, have done what philosophers
have done after him—been carried away by
some meteor of their own forming, or found
their amusement in some of their own intellectual pictures, or palmed some loose and confident
plausibilities of their own upon the world. But
NEWTON *stood true to his principle,* that he would
take up with nothing which wanted evidence,
and he kept by his demonstrations, and his
measurements, and his proofs; and if it be true
that ' he who ruleth his own spirit is greater
than he who taketh a city,' there was won, in
the solitude of his own chamber, many a repeated
victory over himself, which should give a
brighter hue to his name than all the conquests
he has made in the field of discovery, or than
all the splendours of his positive achievements."*

We have only to mention one other sign of
the peculiar kind of superiority with which this

* Dr. Chalmers's "Discourses on the Christian Revelation,
viewed in connexion with the Modern Astronomy," Dis. ii.
p. 60.

extraordinary man was endowed.   He not only
made discoveries himself, but, conscious of the
solidity and the certainty of those discoveries,
he compensated for the brevity of even his long
life, and for the limitation of even his apparently
unbounded powers of thought, by suggesting
the tones of inquiry, and, above all, exemplify-
ing the *true methods* of investigation to all who
have come after him.   The labours of Euler,
Mayer, D'Alembert, La Grange, and Laplace,
in mathematical science; the beautiful discoveries of Herschel, Encke, Bieler, Vermer,
and Adams, in astronomy; the discoveries of
Wollaston, Faraday, Davy, Lavoisier, Gay-
Lussac, Berzelius, in chemistry; the singular
and practically applied investigations of Oersted,
Biot, Savait, and others, in electro-magnetism;
and the brilliant advances made by Frawenhofer,
Young, Brewster, and Faraday, in optics;—all
these may be fairly regarded as the precious
and even propagating fruits of the seeds which
were sown by the master-hand of Newton.
The sublimest conclusion which Newton drew
from his cautious and successful investigations
of the laws of nature, is put, with his characteristic humility, in the form of a "Query."
"These things being rightly described, does it
not appear from the phenomena that there is a

BEING incorporeal, living, intelligent, omnipresent, who, in infinite space, (as it were in
his sensory,) sees the things themselves in-
timately, and thoroughly perceives them, and
comprehends them wholly by their immediate
presence to himself; and of which things the
images only, carried through the organs of sense
into our little sensoriums, are there seen and
beheld by that which in us perceives and
thinks ; and, though every true step made in
this philosophy brings us not immediately to the
knowledge of the First Cause, yet it brings us
nearer to it, and on that account is to be highly
valued." The importance of such a query
from such a man, and at the close of such
demonstrations as he had been giving, will be
best estimated by those who have attentively
considered the poetical and mystic pantheism
which has prevailed for ages in the east, and
which not a few are attempting to substitute, in
our own age and country, for the TRUE and
LIVING GOD—" Of Him, and through Him, and
to Him, are all things : to whom be glory for
ever, Amen," (Rom. xi. 36.)   On this great
subject, we quote the clear and judicious observations of Maclaurin : " As the most obvious
views of the creation suggest to all men the
persuasion of the being and government of a

Deity, so every discovery in natural philosophy enforces it; and with this improvement of his discoveries, this great man concludes both these treatises, ('Principia' and 'Optics.')   Nor is his philosophy to be thought of little service to this purpose, though he has not been able to explain fully the primary causes themselves.

" The great mysterious Being, who made and governs the whole system, has set a part of the chain of causes in our view ; but we find that, as He himself is too high for our comprehension, so his more immediate instruments in the universe are also involved in an obscurity that philosophy is not able to dissipate, and thus our veneration for the supreme Author is always increased in proportion as we advance in the knowledge of his works.   As we arise in philosophy towards the FIRST CAUSE, we obtain more extensive views of the constitution of things, and see his influences more plainly.   We perceive that we are approaching to Him, from the simplicity and generality of the laws that we discover ; from the difficulty we find to account for them mechanically ; from the more and more complete beauty and contrivance that appears to us in the scheme of his works as we advance, and from the hints we obtain of greater things yet out of our reach ; but still we find ourselves at a distance from HIM—the great Source of all motion, power, and efficacy ; who, after all our inquiries, continues removed from us, and veiled in darkness. He is not the object of sense ; his nature and essence are unfathomable ; the more immediate instruments of his power and energy are but obscurely known to us ; the least part of nature, when we endeavour to comprehend it, perplexes us ; even *place* and *time*, of which our ideas seem to be simple and clear, have enough in them to embarrass those who allow nothing to be beyond the reach of their faculties. These things, however, do not hinder, but we may learn to form great and just conceptions of Him from his sensible works, where an art and skill are expressed that is obvious to the most superficial spectator, surprises the most experienced inquirer, and many times surpasses the comprehension of the profoundest philosopher. From what we are able to understand of nature, we may entertain the greater expectations of what will be discovered to us, if ever we shall be allowed to penetrate to the First Cause himself, and see the whole scheme of his works, as they are really derived from him, when our imperfect philosophy shall be completed."

We know from all experience, and from the express revelation of the infinite Creator, that it is not by the investigations of philosophy, however humble, persevering, and successful, that we come to the full knowledge of God, and that it belongs not to our present state of preparation for eternity to receive it. It is gradually revealed, not in his works only, nor even in such a portion of his government as we are able now to trace in the history of man and of the universe, but more gloriously in the gospel of his Son, who is " before all things, and by whom all things consist." The light of that gospel falls on the dark places which human philosophy has never pierced ; it brings out into full splendour and harmony all the attributes of God ; it explains much of the great mystery of being ; and it directs our hopes, on the surest ground, to a future state of light and blessedness, in which the whole scheme of the universe will ever open more widely and more brightly, in ages that have no end. It is here, when philosophy has uttered its last sentence, and breathes its last acknowledgment of ignorance, and weakness, and perplexity, that we learn most seriously the profoundest of the truths which the true philosophy can teach—that God cannot be

discovered *by* man, but must be revealed *to* him.
Hence it is not the mind that either shuns
philosophy, or misapprehends it, or perverts it,
that can derive from it its highest and noblest
teaching ; it is not the arrogant boaster, or the
hasty dealer in conjectures, who has measured
the boundaries of the mind of man ; it is not
the abstract speculator, who imagines that from
the ideas of his own intellect he can work out
a complete system of truth, that is in the right
position for receiving even the elements of
the highest truth ; — but Newton, standing
on the rock of demonstration and experiment, acknowledging that there is a truth
beyond his grasp, and meekly, as a little child,
bowing down his strong, and disciplined, and
triumphant intellect, to receive it from the holy
men inspired of the Holy Ghost to teach it.

It may be imagined that the views of sir
Isaac Newton's superiority to other men, as a
mathematician and as a natural philosopher,
are the exaggerated prejudices of our own
nation.   To prove that this is not the case, we
may quote from two illustrious French writers,
in addition to the testimony of Laplace, which
has been already given.

In the *Eloges* of Fontenelle, on members of
the Royal Academy of Sciences in Paris—of

whom Newton was one—there is an *Eloge* on
our illustrious countryman, occupying more
than thirty octavo pages. Having narrated the
principal events of Newton's life, and reported
his most important discoveries, the eloquent
writer proceeds to say :—

" Newton had the singular felicity of enjoying
the full reward of his merit during his life ;
very different from Descartes, who received
none but posthumous honours. The English
do not honour great talents the less for being
born among themselves. Far from seeking to
abate them by injurious criticisms, far from
applauding the envy which attacks them, they
act in concert to elevate them ; and that grand
liberty which divides them on points the most
important, does not hinder their unity upon
this. They all feel how precious the glory of
intellect ought to be to a state ; and they who
can procure this for their country become infinitely dear to them.

" All the philosophers of a country which has
produced so many, place Newton at their head
by a kind of unanimous acclamation ; they
recognise him as a chief and master. His
philosophy has been adopted through the whole
of England ; it prevails in the Royal Society,
and in all the excellent works which that

Society has published, as already consecrated by
the respect of a long series of ages.   In fine, he
has been revered at the point where death can
bring forth no new honours to him ; he has
seen his apotheosis.   Tacitus, who reproached
the Romans for their indifference to the great
men of their nation, would have praised the
English for the reverse.   In vain would the
Romans have pleaded in excuse, that to them
great merit had become familiar ; Tacitus
would have replied, that great merit never can
be common, or that it was even necessary, if it
were possible, to make it common by the glory
which would be attached to it."[*]

Not less honourable are the praises of
D'Alembert, in the Preliminary Discourse to the
French Encyclopædia : " Newton, for whom the
way had been prepared by Huyghens, at length
appeared, and gave to philosophy a form which
she seems to have been obliged to pursue.   This
great genius saw that it was time to banish conjectures and vague hypotheses from physics, or
at least to allow them no more than their true
value, and that this science ought to be entirely
subjected to the tests of geometry.   It was,
perhaps, with this view that he began by
inventing the ' *Calculus of Infinites*,' and the

----

[*] Œuvres de Fontenelle, tom. vii. pp. 284, 285.

'Method of Consequences,' the use of which,
so extensive in geometry, is still greater for
determining the complicated efforts which are
observed in nature, where everything seems to
be executed by some sorts of infinite progres-
sions. The experiments on gravity, and the
observations of Kepler, discovered to the
English philosopher the force which retains the
planets in their orbits. He learned at once,
both to distinguish the causes of their movements, and to calculate them with an exactitude
which could have been demanded only from the
labour of many ages. The creator of a science
of *optics* entirely new, he showed men light by
decomposing it. All that we could add to the
eulogy of this great philosopher, would be far
below the universal testimony which is rendered
in the present day to his almost innumerable
discoveries, and to his genius, at once extensive,
accurate, and profound. For enriching philosophy with a great quantity of real benefits, he
doubtless merits her acknowledgments ; but he
has, perhaps, done more for her in teaching her
to be wise, and to keep within due bounds that
kind of audacity which circumstances had
forced Descartes to give to her. His theory of
the world (for I do not wish to say his *system*)
is now so generally received, that men begin to

dispute with the author the honour of his invention, because they begin with accusing great
men of deceiving themselves, and finish by
treating them as plagiarists. I leave to those
who find everything in the works of the ancients,
the pleasure of discovering in those works the
gravitation of the planets, though it is not
there ; but even supposing that the Greeks had
the idea,—that which was with them only an
accidental and romantic system, became, in the
hands of Newton, a *demonstration* ; that demonstration, which belongs to him alone, constitutes
the real merit of his discovery ; and *attraction*,
without such a support, would be a hypothesis,
like so many others. If any celebrated writer
should now predict, without any proof, that the
day will come in which gold shall be made,
would our descendants have a right, under that
pretext, to deprive the chemist who actually
does the thing of the honour of a great achieve-
ment ? Does the invention of glasses not belong
to the authors, because some of the ancients
had not thought it impossible that we might,
sometime, extend the sphere of our view ?
Other learned men suppose that they reproach
Newton on better grounds, when they accuse
him of filling his physical science with the
occult qualities of some of the scholastics and

ancient philosophers. But are the learned
persons to whom we refer quite sure that these
two words, without any meaning among the
scholastics, and destined to mark an *essence* of
which they supposed themselves to have the
idea, were intended by the ancient philosophers
to be anything more than a modest expression
of their ignorance? Newton, who had studied
nature, did not flatter himself that he knew
any more than they did of the First Cause
which produced the phenomena; but he did
not use the same language, that he might not
shock his contemporaries, who would not have
failed to attach to them a different idea from
his. He contented himself with proving that
the *whirlpools* of Descartes could not explain
the motions of the planets; that the phenomena and the laws of mechanics united to
overturn them; and that there is one form by
which the planets tend towards each other, the
principle of which is to us entirely unknown.
He did not reject the doctrine of *impulse;* he
confined himself to requiring that it should be
applied more successfully than it had been, for
explaining the motions of the planets. His
desires have not yet been fulfilled, and probably
will not be for a long time. After all, what
harm would he have done to philosophy in

leading us to think that matter may have some properties which we had not suspected, and by disabusing us of our ridiculous confidence that we know all things?"

CHAPTER XII.

It is true of every man, as distinguished from
mere animals, that his real life is within; is the
history of his mind rather than of his body; con-
sisting of his thoughts, affections, motives, and
purposes, and not of the external circumstances
which surround him. Since this is true of every
man, it is so emphatically of the extraordinary
man now before us, of whom it has been elo-
quently said by Dr. Whewell, that " even with
his transcendent powers, to do what he did was
almost irreconcilable with the common conditions of human life, and required the utmost
devotion of thought, energy of effort, and steadi-
ness of will—the strongest character, as well as
the highest endowments, which belong to man."
In tracing the mental life of Newton, it is not
difficult to see from the beginning the faint
outlines which he was continually filling up,
the early play of the mighty mind which

remains " an object of unqualified wonder."
The little manor-house of Woolsthorpe still
bears the almost effaced prediction of his future
greatness in his first attempt at the making of
a dial ; while the relic of another is reverently
preserved by the Royal Society—the gift of one
of its fellows, the rev. Charles Turnor, uncle to
the present owner of the manor. The same
indications assume a clearer and stronger character in the mills, and clocks, and kites, that
amused his companions, who little knew how
vast were the powers and how glorious were
the prospects of the " sober, silent, thinking
lad," who took no pleasure in their common
games. When he left the sheep to stray, and
the cows to tread down the corn, and the honest
servant-man to do the marketing, while he was
solving problems in a hay-loft, or under a hedge,
he was preparing, unconsciously perhaps, for the
gigantic stride which he was afterwards to
make out of the twilight of science into its perfect
day. His vague yearnings after the truth of
judicial astrology led him to those sublime
mathematical studies in which he soon out-
stripped his teachers, and left all other men far
behind him. The prism, which to others
would have been a mere toy, became in his
hands the expounder of the philosophy of

light. To the mechanical act of grinding glasses and constructing telescopes, he gave so much time, that he was considered by many persons on the continent as a maker of telescopes. A person who professed a personal acquaintance with Newton stated, in the " Gentleman's Magazine," many years ago, that one of his philosophical friends abroad sent him a curious prism, which was taken to the customhouse, where sir Isaac claimed it. The officers asked him what its value was, with a view to fixing the duty. The philosopher, who knew more of the laws of the universe than of the laws of duties and drawbacks, simply replied, that the value was so great that he could not ascertain it. They took him at his word, and demanded a most heavy charge, instead of the small duty on a piece of glass according to its weight. And to him, indeed, and through him, to the world, the small piece of glass was of a value beyond all calculation, and was the beginning of a series of inventions, which probably have not yet ended in the magnificent telescope of the earl of Rosse, now the president of the Royal Society ; and by means of these instruments, so delicate, and so difficult of construction, he was able to prove to the senses the truths which he demonstrated by mathema-

tical reasonings to the intellect. In the same
view of the mental life of this great discoverer,
we see the grandeur of thought, the wide sweep
of comprehension, the close and invincible
power of tracing the harmony of seemingly
remote facts:—we see him sitting calmly in his
garden at Woolsthorpe, and connecting so
trivial a circumstance as the fall of an apple
with the revolutions of the heavens. What
serenity as well as power—what intellectual
beauty as well as strength, do we discover in
those abstruse and patient occupations of the
mind, by which he perfected the labours of the
mathematicians who had gone before him, in
the mighty doctrine of fluxions! And, when
he had solved some of the most difficult problems with which the mind of man had grap-
pled, he was so little anxious for the honour
with which these operations have adorned his
memory, that, by his delay in publishing them,
that honour, which might have been his own,
is now divided with a rival. Though he was
called away from his beloved retirement at
Cambridge, to defend the independence of the
university and the dignity of British law, before
the High Commission, and afterwards in Parliament, his mind was still absorbed in the lofty
pursuits of science, and he may be truly said to

have *lived* in his study all the time. **Newton**
would have been more than a man, if he had
been insensible to the obscurity and compara-
tive poverty in which, for many years, he was
permitted to live. It appears from many parts
of his correspondence, that he had reason to
complain of the neglect with which he was
treated in high quarters. We are not in
possession of all the circumstances which
eventually led his friend Montague to secure
his promotion to the mastership of the Mint;
nor does it appear in what way he accumu-
lated so large a fortune as that which he left
behind him, or why he did not become a bene-
factor, as Hearne reported he had promised, to
the Royal Society. Among the papers of the
Royal Society, there is a curious note of Newton's, accompanied by a letter from Dr. Wollaston, from which it appears that, like other
eminent men of his day, Newton was a holder
of South Sea Stock, which he bought in 1720,
for £650; it amounted fourteen months after
to more than £21,000; and it was sold apparently at a loss, not long before the scheme
exploded, plunging thousands into irretrievable
ruin, from which ruin even the Bank of England
had a narrow escape.

" Dr. Wollaston, to whom the Society are

indebted for this very interesting autograph note, observes, in his letter accompanying it, that not knowing any such occurrence in the life of Newton had ever been made public, he was for many years unwilling to divulge the transaction ; but having since found that the losses which Newton sustained by the South Sea scheme have been noticed in the biographical memoir drawn up on the authority of Mr. Conduit, he no longer hesitates to present the document, being satisfied that it will be considered by every reflecting mind, an instructive instance of the soundest understanding being liable to have its judgment perverted by the appearance of enormous profit, and to forget that such profit can only be aimed at with proportionate risk of failure." *

In such transactions, which have become familiar to the present generation, we probably can be sure of nothing else than of Newton's participation in the natural and common desire for gain, which is dishonourable only when it is excessive, or when it stoops to means of gratification which are opposed to the will of God. Yet it is not without instruction, that in this particular, as in many others, intellectual

* "History of the Royal Society," by C. R. Weld, Esq., vol. i. p. 440.

eminence confers no exemption from the ordinary cares and vulgar infirmities of mortals. Nor is it out of place to remind the reader, that " they that *will* be rich fall into temptation and a snare."

In this memoir of sir Isaac Newton, the YOUNG may see to whom they are indebted, as the servant of Providence, for opening to them the most enchanting fields of science, and the most splendid demonstrations of philosophy. From him they learn, not only a great body of facts, and the connexion of those facts in the boundless works of God, but, what is still more precious, the kind of thinking by which these glorious discoveries are to be appreciated and enjoyed. It is not by the dreams of imagination, nor by indolently taking every truth upon trust, but by calm inquiry, patient investigation, and humble reception of whatever is *proved to be true*, that they can arise to the contemplation of the Creator's works. This ought to be, and with very many it is, a motive for submitting to those severe studies by which the intellect is tasked, yet disciplined, strengthened, and improved, and thus prepared for understanding the greatest productions of the noblest minds, and the infinitely glorious manifestations of the wisdom and the power of God.

The *results* of Newton's philosophy have been

set forth by many writers in the most popular and pleasing style; but it belongs to that higher education, which is increasingly prized among all classes, to become familiar with the practical experiments, and even with the geometrical reasonings, which prove that this philosophy is undoubtedly true. We may not expect often, if ever, again to behold a man of equal powers of mind with Newton; yet we may hope to see thousands and tens of thousands who can appreciate his discoveries, because *they understand them for themselves*. It seems to be the plan of Him who made us, who created the vast universe, and who has endowed us with faculties for beholding him by means of the material creation, that, by seeing how widely we are separated from the shining worlds whose motions and whose laws prove them to belong to the same system as our own, we should be led to think of another state of being, in which the knowledge we have gained here is to be enlarged, and where the mysteries that now surround us shall be among the most familiar of our thoughts. It is thus that our knowledge grows in this life, not so much by becoming acquainted with *new objects*, as by being able to connect them with what we knew before, perceiving in what respects they agree, and in

what respects they differ. The more knowledge we really have, the more precious every
new acquisition becomes. And if it be so, as
assuredly it is, in the experience of this world,
what a bright and intelligible prospect is opened
before us into the world of which it is said,
" That which is in part shall be done away,"
and where, instead of seeing as now " through
a glass darkly," we " shall know as we are
known," and shall see " face to face." Other,
and sublimer, and holier contemplations of
God, indeed, belong to the intellectual employments of eternity ; and with these contemplations, not of philosophy, but of religion—not of
sense, but of faith—not of reason, but of actual
experience — we must become familiar on
earth, as a necessary preparation for heaven.
Still, as the God who reveals his grace in our
salvation is the same God whom David adored
amidst the lights of the starry firmament, the
ever-unfolding mystery of Eternal Love will
include the whole of that Divine method of
self-manifestation which constitutes the real
history of the universe. There is, therefore, a
most pious and spiritual use to which we may
apply the expansion of the intellect by the discoveries of philosophy, sinking in humility as
we rise in understanding, and feeling more of

the reverence of seraphim as we approach
more nearly to that THRONE, before which they
veil their wings and utter their adorations.

And since it seems to be His own ordination
that the light of knowledge should thus gradually shine into our minds, how unspeakably
important is it that, in the study of the earth
and the heavens, and the laws of their num-
berless and complicated movements, we should
be ever mindful of the Presence in which we
live, of the Power by which we move, of the
Goodness in which we have our being! And
since the study of these " natural" objects
brings our intellectual capacity so near to the
truth concerning God, what words can describe
the immeasurably higher claims of those "spiritual" things, which have to do with our own
undying nature, with our moral relation to
God, with our departure from him by sin, and
with our restoration to him by his grace,
through his incarnate Son. It was not to teach
philosophy, *nor to disparage it*, that " he was
manifest," but " to take away our sins," and by
the righteousness of his holy life, and the atone-
ment of his sacrificial death, to reconcile us to
God. The glory of that Divine Saviour is so
represented to us in the New Testament, that
the more we understand of the works of God,

the more completely do we enter into the inspired descriptions of his grandeur, and feel the glowing energy of those praises with which apostles crown him. As he walked this earth, which he himself had made, and worked in the daylight of that sun whose brightness he had kindled, he displayed the majesty of God in the tenderness of man, and poured out his tears and blood, that at his cross man might meet his God in peace, and then go forth to study all the works of God, and to do all his will, in the free spirit of adoption.

> " The soul that sees Him, or receives, sublimed,
> New faculties, or learns at least to employ
> More worthily the powers he own'd before,
> Discerns in all things what, with stupid gaze
> Of ignorance, till then he overlook'd—
> A ray of heavenly light, gilding all forms
> Terrestrial in the vast and the minute—
> The unambiguous footsteps of the God
> Who gives its lustre to an insect's wing,
> And wheels his throne upon the rolling worlds."*

It would be a great oversight for any young person to read the Life of Newton, without learning what a foolish mistake it is to imagine that genius is idle, impulsive, eccentric, raised above the necessity of observing the vulgar rules of order and propriety. It is true, *shamefully* true, we may say, that there have been too many instances in which highly-gifted men

* Cowper's Task, book v.

have exhibited the weakness or the wayward-ness of setting at naught the ties of family, the courtesies of life, and even the plain commands of God. But it is an impertinence to call these follies or sins the accompaniments of genius. No powers of reasoning, of imagina-tion, or of action, can raise any human being *above* the dignity of rectitude; and it is no proof of genius to sink *below* it. We believe that the fond admiration of the imperfections and inconsistencies of great men is passing away, with many other absurdities. In the name of the immortal Newton, confessedly the most exalted genius of modern Europe, we rebuke it.

We need scarcely urge another considera-tion, which cannot fail to commend itself to every intelligent reader of this Life—the wide difference between mere speculation and true philosophy. It was by *refusing to speculate* that Newton learned to philosophize. There are, indeed, innumerable speculations now afloat on almost every subject. Some of them are, probably, nearer the truth than others; and there are, doubtless, not a few advan-tages, to certain classes of minds, in pursuing them, and bringing them to the test of dis-ciplined reason; but they are *not* philosophy; they are notions, not things. Sometimes they are merely the notions entertained by some minds concerning the notions of other minds—shadows of clouds. The path to true philosophy is humbler, more difficult, but it leads to real and unquestionable truth. It is not amusement, but labour; not guessing, but knowledge; not reasoning out a scheme of things that *ought to be*, but a *finding out* of things that *are*. Such is the crowning honour that belongs to Newton. He was a philosopher. His department was the material creation. There are other departments—the mind, and the objects with which the mind is conversant without the bodily senses—spirits—heaven—God; but it is only by applying to these departments the same rigid method of demanding proof—suitable and sufficient proof—that the human mind can attain to any results deserving to be called philosophy.

It is our hope that this Life of Newton will engage the attention of not a few PARENTS. To them, we think, it is rich in suggestions, in cautions, and in encouragements. Here a child, left without a father, whose mother, struggling with but comparatively scanty means, might at one time have looked upon herself as peculiarly unhappy in having a

son who appeared so unlikely to be fitted for
the duties of the station in which he was born.
Yet she had discernment as well as affection,
and she wisely yielded to the manifest designs
of Providence, by obtaining the best guidance
and culture for such mental powers and tastes
as were indicated by her weakly boy. Un-
happily, we have no record of that mother's
mode of dealing with him. But it would be
unjust to her memory not to suppose that she
fostered in his young heart that love of truth,
that rectitude of principle, that wise benevolence, and, above all, that reverence for God,
and that deep attachment to the Scriptures, as
well as to nature, which formed his character
through life. The mothers of boys remarkable
for their intellectual power and activity, have
indeed a most precious charge committed to
them, and on their wisdom and piety it is
impossible to say how much depends.

It is not the natural tendency of parents to
think too lightly of the abilities of their children ; yet the number is, probably, not great,
of those who take the pains to estimate such
abilities aright, and to meditate on the particular course which it is right and safe to
pursue in training them. In that middle class
of English society to which the family of

Newton belonged, there is great danger of
sacrificing some of the dearest interests of
humanity to the one ambition of acquiring
wealth. But there is something richer than
wealth, ay, even in this life. To have an
expanded, disciplined, and cultivated mind—
to be able to look with intelligence and religious
adoration on the varieties of beings and relations
that fill the earth and the heavens—to provide
intellectual food and delight for the millions of
human beings that come, in rapid succession,
into this world as a school of instruction, a field
of labour, a scene of moral trial, and a course
of preparation for futurity—these are grander
acquisitions than wealth, and such as wealth
can never purchase. We look to the great
rehearsal of life in the nursery, to the gentle
leadings of parental love, to the prudent and
tender nurture of early years, for the elevation
of a large and most important class of our
countrymen above the universal and absorbing
thirst for gain. We do not expect a Newton in
every manor-house ; but we may look in every
family raised above the lowest range of poverty,
and in many even of tha lowest range, for the
tastes that will prepare the nascent mind of
England for similar studies, and for the mental
discipline which will insure a higher training

in the school or in the college. It is very much
with a view to the awakening of such desires
in the hearts of parents, that we have put
together the facts and the meditations of this
little book. We know that, except in strongly
marked cases, like that of Newton, there is no
incompatibility between the pursuits of agricul-
ture or of trade, or any of the professions, to
which the youth of our land are aspiring, and
the kind of intellectual preparation for the
active employments of life which we now
recommend. For want of such ennobling
habits as are secured by the regulation of the
whole mind—the practical love of truth, virtue,
and religion—a large portion of the men around
us have no resource, when not occupied with
their daily business, but the gratification of the
appetites, or the frivolous amusements of the
age. This would not be, if *boyhood* were more
reverenced by parents, and if more thought and
pious care were directed to the kindling of
nobler desires, and the implanting of higher
principles at the beginning. Why should not
every boy be taught to revere the name of
Newton, to understand the reasons for that
reverence, to emulate the example here set
before him? And, if this were done, would
there not be a grace and beauty worthy of

universal admiration, in the very persons who, otherwise become the mere drudges of the farm, the market, or the factory? There is more delight experienced, too, in the pursuits of science, even as a relaxation, than in the charms of poetry, or romance, or song; and the more dignified entertainment of the intellect is a much better refreshment of the faculties amidst the ordinary work of life.

But we plead for science, philosophy, the study of the works of God, on their own merits. They are known, by all who cherish them, to be worthy, in themselves, of all the attention they receive. They more than repay the labour by the fruit. They need not be costly. In the present day, the publications which meet the wants of the young in this respect are less expensive than any other means of gratification. The apparatus for making experiments in natural philosophy, in optics, in chemistry, and even in astronomy, are brought within the reach of all. Neither is it requisite that time should be improperly taken from the more pressing claims which the situation of young men imposes; for few are so entirely taken up with those peculiar duties as to have no leisure at command, and it is for the devotion of a portion of that leisure to such pursuits that we ask leave to plead.

Neither is there ground for apprehending that
the occupation of youthful minds with the works
of God, and with the writings of such authors as
most accurately and fully expound them, is necessarily fraught with the danger of withdrawing
them from the word of God, and the exercises
of devotion ; on the contrary, the more intelligent the devotion, the greater is the security for
its being conscientious, habitual, and persevering—at an equal distance from superstitious
formality and from supercilious unbelief; and
the more truly evangelical and spiritual the
worship of the heart, the stronger is the motive
for seeking to know as much as may be known
of Him to whom that worship is humbly, grate-
fully, believingly presented.

If the parents of the generation that is rising up
neglect what we believe to be their duty in these
matters, let them not wonder if their sons become
mere worldlings, or something worse. The times
are changing; mind is more active. The allure-
ments which appeal to the senses are more
refined. The moving of the passions through
the imagination is becoming more subtle ; and
the literature which prostitutes the most
dazzling genius to the basest ends, is borne, as
it were, by every breeze to every door. We
know of no human counteraction of these bale-

ful seductions, so congenial with the spirit of
that religion which is the shield of Heaven
against all the temptations that assail the young,
as the enlightening, bracing, exalting, and
attractive studies which are embodied in the
name of Newton.

We anticipate some objection to this line of
remark from those who are sincerely jealous
on behalf of pure and simple Christianity. It
would not express our view to ascribe this jealousy to prejudice. Still, we must account this
particular form of that jealousy as an error. To
none do we yield, we trust, in earnest zeal for
the gospel, as the living and practical faith of
Christians. Not for an hour would we give way
to the advocates of any system by which *that*
would be endangered. But is the gospel consistent with studying anything else besides the
Scriptures—with doing anything besides the
things which are required of Christian wor-
shippers as peculiarly spiritual duties ? Is the
belief of any truth discordant with the belief of
the truth taught by inspiration ? These questions can receive but one answer. Ignorance,
mental lethargy, the neglect of what belongs to
us as men, as citizens, and as beings endowed
with unmeasured capacities, placed in the
boundless universe of the infinite Creator—are

no part of Christianity, are not countenanced by Jesus Christ, are not consistent with the thorough working out of his religion. Then, surely, all that is precious and Divine in that system which is all precious, because all Divine, would rather urge than hinder the utmost possible improvement, the most exalted and intense activity of the powers by which God has raised us above the brutes that perish. Such an error as that against which we here protest, might have suited the dark ages of Europe, and may be in harmony with every superstition which *dreads the light.* But, among Protestant Christians, in a land on which her Newton has shed more glory than all her statesmen, merchants, or princes, let it be universally and evermore denounced. We need not be reminded that science does not show the way to heaven—that philosophy cannot save the soul—that it would be possible to have the genius and intelligence of Newton even, and yet be far from God. It will not be *proved* to us that there is more peril in studying astronomy than in cultivating fields, in keeping shops, in buying and selling, in eating, drinking, and sleeping, and doing the drudgery of vulgar life.

It may be hoped that enough has been said to disabuse the minds of such as may be hovering on the borders of error on this subject; on those who are so confirmed in it that it has become a part of their religious system, we have no expectation that anything we can say will produce the least impression. But we are thankful to know that there is a large, and, happily, increasing number of parents who know better, who have learned, both from observation and from experience, that there is no real opposition between true science and pure religion. To them the life of Newton suggests innumerable lessons. It encourages them to mingle in the instructions which they give to their children, or procure for them, the harmonious exhibition of all the truth which God is teaching, whether by his works or in his words.

We venture a word or two to CHRISTIANS. It is for them to give encouragement to every wise and well-conducted attempt to break down the wall which has been built between knowledge and devoutness, between the free and noble pursuits of science and the humble and obedient spirit of faith. What the Newtonian philosophy has done for man in relation to the physical creation, the liberty won by reformers from an usurping church has done for man in relation to the spiritual realities discovered by the gospel. If

the right to read the Bible is to be intelligently
maintained, it must be by maintaining, at the
same time, the kindred right to read what
God has written on the earth and on the
heavens, and on all things visible ; and the
true worth of our intellectual freedom from
human authority in the study of the Scriptures
is never fully appreciated but by those who
taste the sweets, and reap the fruits, of that
freedom in the study of nature.   Unless it is
imagined that He who inspired the prophets
and apostles does not guide the stars in the
firmament, nor fill the world with riches, nor
cover the earth with forests, and flowers, and
harvests, and living beings—it *must* be seen
that the message of revelation acquires a deeper
meaning, a more defined authority, a more
thrilling interest, for minds that are already
conversant with the majesty of God, which fills
all space and all ages.   If there were nothing
to extend the human mind in science, nothing
to regale the intellect, to adorn the imagination,
or to delight the heart in the minute or magnificent contemplations of science, it would still
deserve to be pursued, in all its varied ramifi-
cations, for the testimony which it bears to the
great truth on which religion builds its doctrines, its institutions, and its hopes—*the ever-*

present and ever-working GOD; and for the illustration which it gives of the grand evangelical assertion—that He who claims our confidence and our obedience as our Saviour and our Lord, is the Maker and Proprietor of all things. The more we know of the things which God has made, and of the wise and simple laws by which he orders all their relations and all their movements, the larger is the meaning which we attach to the entire message of the gospel, and the more intelligent is our conviction that the doctrine is not of man but of God. We acknowledge, indeed, readily and with gratitude, that the essentials of the Bible, its saving truths, its gracious promises, its practical directions, are apprehended by minds unvisited by science; but such minds, if enlightened by exact knowledge of the works and ways of God in nature, would see in all that they have hitherto believed a fuller glory, and find in all that has been most dear to them a new charm. Thus, instead of leaving the paths of science to be trodden only by those who are strangers to the grace of God, and who are tempted to depreciate the faith of Christians because they take no interest in such sublime discoveries as Newton's, it were better for the interests of Christianity, not less than of science, for those who know the gospel to tread these paths themselves, and to show the unbelieving or the indifferent companions of their walks, that science, pursued aright, and to its legitimate ends, becomes religion, and that the most fitting contemplation of this universe of wonders is in the attitude of faith, and in hymns of praise. It is because Christians acknowledge the duty of carrying their principles into the world of business and of social life, that they become " the salt of the earth." When they carry the same principles into the world of science and the companion- ship of philosophy, what are they but " the light of the world?"

The intellect of man, quite as much as his practical working, needs the presence of those who, while engaged in the same employment as others, teach by their example the manifold applications of that grand lesson, which all but Christians are neglecting, (and which some Christians, even, might remember more continually,) " Whatsoever ye do, do all to the glory of God."

To the disciples of Newton, the lovers of science for its own sake, and for the sake of its bearings on the works of man, we may be allowed to say—Do not stop short at the experiments, the reasonings, the *material* uses of his

glorious philosophy. Look to the beginning.
Look to the end. Consider what a mind that
was which has taught you so much, and what
a mind your own is which is capable of receiving and applying such noble truths. Then
follow Newton from his laboratory to his closet—
from the stars of light to the God who fixed
their orbits and who gave them laws—from the
discovery of truth in the things that are seen,
to the revelation of truth in the " things that are
not seen." If the true philosophy is, as we
know it to be, in harmony with the true religion—and if the pursuits of physical science can
be, and ought to be, subservient to the higher
relations which connect us with God and
with eternity—it is equally true that religion
is in harmony with philosophy, that the
gospel sheds a holy light on every walk of
science, adding new zest to its discoveries, and,
when those discoveries are felt to be exhausted
by the limitation of our powers, putting into
our hands a higher *calculus*, and a more widely
reaching method, that, walking by faith, we
may commune with God :—ascending that path
on which the most intelligent traveller is he
whose reliance on his guide is most simple,
where the most costly offering is presented
with the most grateful heart, and the highest of

the sons of men is the humblest of the sons of God. How beautiful is harmony! How admirable is proportion! How satisfying is the demonstration of law! If it be so on earth, what must it be in heaven—where the harmony of all the works and ways of God, the moral proportions of his government, and the perfect working of the law of love, will be the contemplation, the experience, and the bliss of all the saved!

ALSO AVAILABLE FROM ATTIC BOOKS